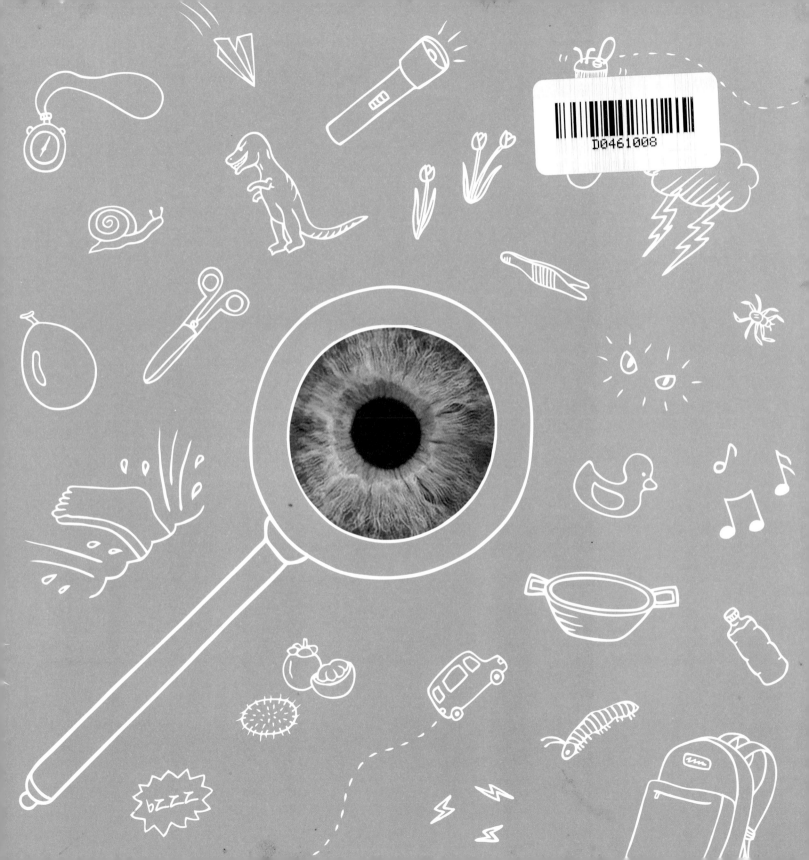

exploralab

150+ Ways to Investigate the Amazing Science All Around You

Contents

LAB 01
Open Your Eyes

LAB 02
Who's That in the Mirror?

LAB 08
Windows and Weather

LAB 09
That Big Patch of Grass

LAB 10
All Around Your Downtown

LAB 11
Wonder About the Water

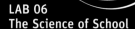

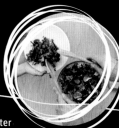

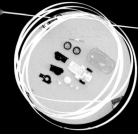

Welcome to *Exploralab*

This book is a journey through your daily life—from waking up in the morning to hitting the sack at night, and all the mini-adventures you encounter in between! Each lab—based on activities and exhibits pioneered by the Exploratorium in San Francisco—highlights a single moment in the day that's rich with scientific wonder. The activities within each lab help you explore the fascinating science happening all around you, morning, noon, and night.

Science isn't found only in laboratories filled with test tubes and computers, or even in classrooms filled with textbooks and math quizzes. Instead it lives and breathes in everything you see and do, from walking down a city street to swinging on a tree branch to playing pick-up B-ball with friends. You're eating breakfast? You can learn about everything from fluid dynamics to magnetism right at the table—and have a pretty sweet time doing it, too. Hanging out before bedtime? You can travel to the stars, dodge monsters, and learn to see in the dark without ever leaving your own backyard.

Everyone is a scientist, and you, as a kid, are among the best scientists of all. Don't believe us? Your head is like a sponge (an especially good-looking sponge, of course) that soaks up information about the world and its workings at home, at school, on the bus, at the beach, and everywhere else you go. All you need to do is keep your eyes open, your curiosity honed sharp as a samurai's sword, and your questions at the ready.

The smartest scientists sometimes ask the seemingly simplest questions—like, why do we stick to the ground rather than float away into space? Why does the Moon go around the Earth and not vice versa?—and those simple questions often lead to profound answers. Ask why stuff works the way it does and exactly what's happening under the surface of things you see and do every day. Nothing's off limits in this book, or in your new life as Kid Scientist, PhD.

So go ahead. Your day—and all the moments in your day—is like a pirate's treasure chest filled with funky, weird, funny, and unexpected new knowledge. Grab a key, open the lock, and see what's inside.

How to Use This Book

This book is meant to be carried around as you go through your day. When you get curious about something you see, pull it out and use it as an experiment guide. And riff on stuff, too: If you want to explore a subject the book doesn't cover, find a related activity and hack its instructions until it fits your needs.

LABS:
From morning yawns to lights out, each lab offers experiments to run, games to play, and puzzles to solve, all linked to parts of your day. Some also have special gizmos for you to explore!

YOU'LL NEED:
Everything you need to do an activity is listed inside these circles.

WHAT'S THE DEAL?:
These circles give you the low-down on the facts behind the fun, explaining the physical laws and weird science underlying the book's activities.

MAGNIFYING GLASS:
Pull out the book's magnifier for a close-up look at the materials used in these activities.

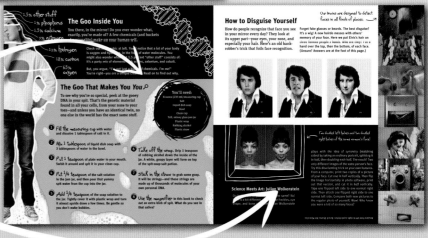

SCIENCE MEETS ART:
Meet artists who mix scientific principles, natural materials and processes, and a lot of curiosity to create works that show us the world in fresh, funny, and surprising ways.

Tool Kit

A handful of basic stuff—which is probably lying around your home right now—helps you do the activities in this book. Stick them in your backpack so they'll be right there when you need them.

CHEAP WATERPROOF CAMERA

GLUE

MAGNIFIER (THE ONE IN THIS BOOK OR A STRONG HAND LENS)

SCISSORS

CLEAR TAPE

MEASURING CUPS AND SPOONS

PAPER, PENCILS (COLORED AND REGULAR), AND CHALK

PLIERS

TWEEZERS

STOPWATCH OR WRISTWATCH WITH SECOND HAND

MEASURING TAPE

LOTS OF FRIENDS OR FAMILY MEMBERS TO EXPERIMENT ON

Look Around

List questions, record results, and sketch scenes in a lab book—here are several great types to try.

You need head tools as well as hand tools to use this book (and to move beyond the book to create your own experiments). Don't worry—they're already packed away in your brain.

WEEKLY PLANNER

MON 4/15: tomato seeds are sprouting!

TUE 4/16: buds showing up on stems.

WED

A calendar with spaces to record daily observations

LOOK AT WHAT OTHER PEOPLE DON'T
Sometimes we trundle through life without wondering why the sky's blue or why the stars shine at night. Explorers like you, though, stop to look, ask questions, and figure out why ordinary stuff is actually pretty extraordinary.

TOUCH WHAT OTHER PEOPLE WON'T
To be a scientist, you gotta get your hands dirty. And wet. And sticky. There's lots to learn from saliva, snot, bugs, and mud. Wear gloves when you need to, but pick up and poke around in the things that make you curious.

TEST YOUR GUESSES
Before you try out an activity, ask yourself what you think the result will be. What evidence leads you to that guess? Afterward, if the result's not what you predicted, what should you do? Redo the activity, and figure out why!

A tablet device with a lab-book app for easy data input

BRING LAB PARTNERS
Science is twice the fun with two people, three times the fun with three. And with a crowd, it's practically a party. Friends and family can be your test subjects, they can hold stuff for you, and they can point out your epic fails and cheer your epic wins. So bring them along!

WRITE IT DOWN
Facts and figures fall out of even the smartest brain when that brain's owner forgets to write them down. When you measure, weigh, or time something in an activity, record the results in a lab book (see the list at right) so you can refer to them later.

DITCH THIS BOOK
Like any book, this one's only a launch pad. Read it, try its activities on for size, and then put it down to investigate the world outside its pages. You'll carry its lessons with you as you invent new, bigger, radder experiments that reveal the world to you and your friends.

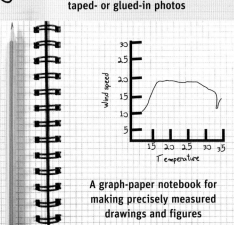

toadstools on log by the river!

one day the caterpillar on the porch turned into a butterfly!

A durable, hard-backed lined journal for field notes and taped- or glued-in photos

A Word for Parents

The activities in this book are designed for kids eight and older. The Exploratorium and the publisher have made every effort to ensure the information and instructions included here are accurate, reliable, and mind-blowingly cool, but keep your own child's skills and attention span in mind before allowing him or her to try them, and provide supervision as needed. We disclaim all liability for any unintended, unforeseen, or improper application of the suggestions in this book, as well as any stained T-shirts and soggy sneakers. We're happy to accept credit for your kid's ever-increasing awesomeness, of course.

A graph-paper notebook for making precisely measured drawings and figures

About the Exploratorium

Since Frank Oppenheimer opened up the museum in 1969, we've been an interactive learning lab—a hands-on, playful place to discover and to tinker—and our creative, thought-provoking activities and programs have ignited curiosity and delighted visitors. Here are just a few of the "please touch!" exhibits inside our doors.

Think with your hands in activities that ask you to slow down, roll up your sleeves, build your own playful contraptions, and invent your own experiments.

Pendulum snake

Pixel Wall

Experiment with light, color, sound, and motion through dozens of ears-and-eyes-open activities that let you play with the way you hear and see the world. Create giant soap bubbles, crawl through the Tactile Dome, dance with your shadow, or climb inside a huge kaleidoscope.

Exhibits created by artists bring scientific principles to life and spur questions about why we create art and how it help us to learn about the physical world.

Soap Film Painting

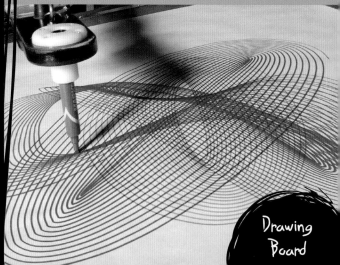

Drawing Board

Giant mirror

ook at yourself in a completely new way in exhibits that turn you upside-down
nd spin you around. Then explore how your own mind works and investigate the
cientific study of human behavior through experiments in emotion, language,
emory, and pattern recognition.

Vanity mirror

Plankton Populations

Discover parts of the natural world that you normally
can't see, and use scientific tools to learn about hard-to-
see living things, the ecosystems they inhabit, and the
processes they share.

Gyroid

Watch shifting winds and tides, observe human behavior,
and find new ways to notice the places we inhabit at the
Bay Observatory Gallery and the Outdoor Gallery, key
parts of our new home on San Francisco's Pier 15.

Open Your Eyes

Dawn is spreading over the horizon. Light is pouring into the room. So open your eyes, your ears, and all of your senses to learn the secrets of the early AM world.

Here comes the Sun! It's traveled 93,435,000 miles (105,700,00 Km) from the depths of space all the way to your sleepy face.

Birds wake up way too early. Can you guess what they're singing about? And which other noises can you hear?

ring! ring!

If your alarm clock's annoying you, break it! Then see what's inside.

Check that halitosis! Learn how to tell when your breath smells like a beast's... and why.

Why are your eyelids glued together? The sandman's visited you in the night.

Your eyes are haunted—not by ghosts, but by spooky afterimages and phosphenes that put on light shows inside your eyelids.

Where Does Light Come From?

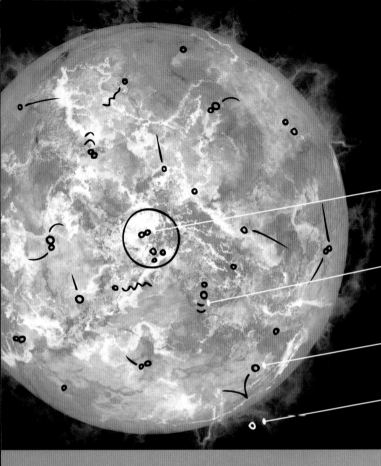

Hey, you—pull your head out from under that pillow and say hi to the sunshine! It's journeyed a long way to wake you up today.

Long before human civilization began, a *photon* (packet of electromagnetic energy) was born deep in the nuclear furnace of the Sun's core...

slammed into charged particles deep inside the Sun at 186,411 miles per second (300,000 km/s) for 10,000 to 270,000 years...

reached the Sun's surface after 435,000 miles (700,000 km)...

escaped in the form of light and heat...

Knock Apart Your Clock

Did your alarm clock razz you out of sweet, sweet dreams this AM? Take revenge by taking that thing to pieces and finding out how it ticks and tocks.

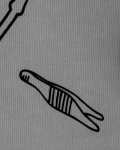

1 First get your parents' okay to break the clock, then unplug it and remove all batteries. Collect a small screwdriver, tweezers, pliers, and other tools that will help you pry and spy.

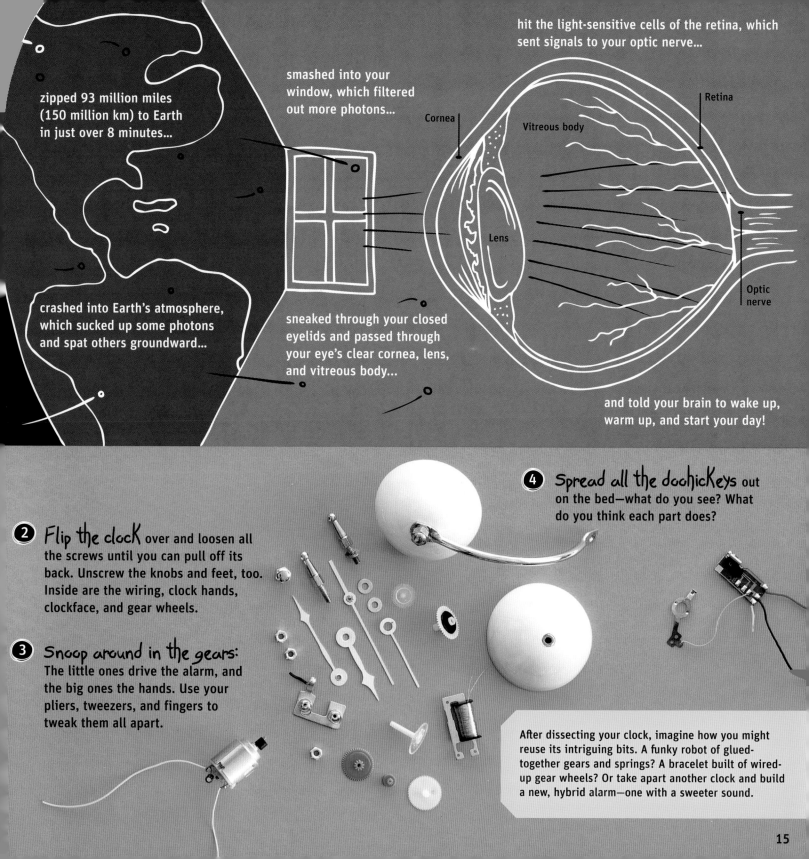

zipped 93 million miles (150 million km) to Earth in just over 8 minutes...

crashed into Earth's atmosphere, which sucked up some photons and spat others groundward...

smashed into your window, which filtered out more photons...

sneaked through your closed eyelids and passed through your eye's clear cornea, lens, and vitreous body...

hit the light-sensitive cells of the retina, which sent signals to your optic nerve...

Cornea

Vitreous body

Retina

Lens

Optic nerve

and told your brain to wake up, warm up, and start your day!

② **Flip the clock** over and loosen all the screws until you can pull off its back. Unscrew the knobs and feet, too. Inside are the wiring, clock hands, clockface, and gear wheels.

③ **Snoop around in the gears:** The little ones drive the alarm, and the big ones the hands. Use your pliers, tweezers, and fingers to tweak them all apart.

④ **Spread all the doohickeys** out on the bed—what do you see? What do you think each part does?

After dissecting your clock, imagine how you might reuse its intriguing bits. A funky robot of glued-together gears and springs? A bracelet built of wired-up gear wheels? Or take apart another clock and build a new, hybrid alarm—one with a sweeter sound.

Ghosts Get in Your Eyes

Afterimages—the blurry blobs you spot after staring at something for a while—are like phantoms. They exist only in your eyes and brain, but they sure do *look* real. Run an experiment to understand how this colorful phenomenon works.

Stare at the center of the blue basketball on the orange banner here for 15 to 20 seconds. Then focus on the middle of the white banner. You'll see a faint blue afterimage (with an orange ball and border) for a moment. It will quickly fade. Try the same experiment in your room, staring at a blue picture or poster, and then switching your gaze to a blank wall. This time, a red phantom will show up!

What's the Deal?

Your eyes contain light-sensitive *cone* cells in three varieties, each of which picks up a different hue. When you tire out the cones that see one color, such as red, they don't work when you look away at the white banner. So green- or blue-sensitive cones kick in until the red cones recover and get back in the game. Boo: a blue ghost!

The Sandman's Presents

The sandman's not a nice guy like the tooth fairy. Instead of shiny coins, he leaves you bits of icky dried-up eyelid goo. This stuff, which scientists call *gound* and everyone else calls "eye boogers" or "sleepers," is a soup of mucus, oil, and dead skin and blood cells that your eyes naturally produce all day long.

When you're awake, you just blink it away. But you don't blink while you sleep, so it clumps up into gritty particles. A cold or allergies makes the sandman's presents nastier still: Your sinuses are connected to your tear ducts, providing extra mucus for him to paste on your sleepy eyelids. Yuck!

Morning Monster Breath

There's no mystery about why morning breath is monstrous: Your mouth gets less oxygen and makes less spit at night, so bacteria have themselves a big ol' stinky jamboree in there.

It's hard to know when you have dragon breath because your nose is used to your own body odors. But a few tricks can reset your smell sense and tell you if you're blowing out fumes.

Gently rub the back of your tongue with a cotton swab or toothpick. Set it aside for a minute. Then smell it. Nothing? You're golden.

Breathe into your pillowcase or a handkerchief. Let it sit for a moment, and then take a good long sniff of the fabric.

Still unsure if you stink? Go breathe on your brother. He'll tell you the truth.

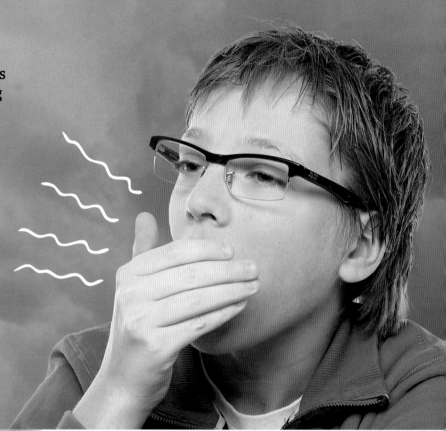

Phantasmagoric Phosphenes

One of the first things you do after waking up is rub your drowsy eyes. The result: a private fireworks show across the backs of your eyelids.

The dancing dots and spirals you see when you press on your eyelids are called *phosphenes.* Pressure fools cells in the retina, at the back of your eye, to fire and send messages to your brain that say, "Hey, lots of light in here!" Usually you see phosphenes only in complete darkness, as is the case when your eyes are closed.

Long ago, phosphenes were called "prisoners' cinema" because they entertained inmates held in dark cells. A whack to the head—or even a whomping big sneeze—can trigger a phosphene show, too, which is why stars and lightning bolts always circle around cartoon creatures' heads after they get bonked on the noggin.

17

Throw a Yawn Party

Once you're out of bed, lasso some family members and pets, and start a yawn riot in your house.

1 Yawn as widely and noisily as you can while everybody watches you.

2 See who yawns back. Dad? The baby? (He'll probably ignore you.) The dog? (He might not.)

3 Look around to check whether your yawn is spreading throughout the room. Can anyone resist?

What's the Deal?

People once thought a yawn meant you were sleepy and needed extra oxygen. Then scientists gave people pure oxygen to breathe and saw they still did it. We don't know exactly why we need to stretch our jaws like this, but we do know that yawns spread like wildfire—watch someone do it and you'll probably do it, too. (Kids don't "catch" yawns until they're about six years old, though.) Even some animals do it socially—a dog sees another one yawn, and soon there's a yawn party on the lawn.

Lend Your Ears a Hand

Spy on all the sounds inside—and outside—your house in the morning with your own homemade hearing aid.

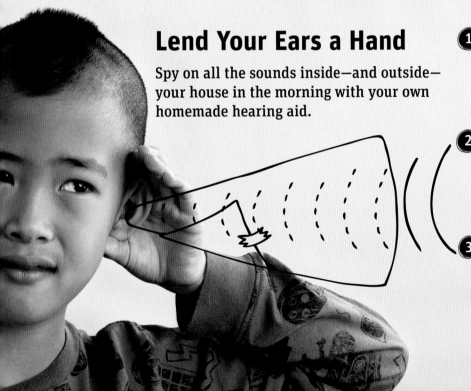

1 Listen to the morning's noises without leaving the room to see what's making them. What do you hear? Do you think that's bacon sizzling or water running? Could that be a woodpecker in the yard, or is it a construction crew at work?

2 Cup your hand around the back of one ear. Those mysterious sounds get louder because you've enhanced all the natural noise-focusing whorls of your outer ear, which are designed to funnel noise toward the ear canal and then to the eardrum.

3 Roll a sheet of paper into a cone shape and tape it together. Gently place its small end at your ear canal's opening and turn the wide-open end toward your bedroom window or door. Now you should able to tell what, exactly, is making all that racket!

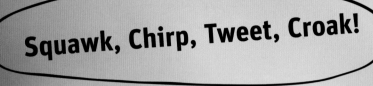

Squawk, Chirp, Tweet, Croak!

There's nothing like a pack of chatty birds to jar you awake—even before the Sun's up. What are all those birds yakking about? Eavesdrop on them with a bedside bird-babble journal.

Write down your description of the sound you hear, whether it's a croak or a pleasant trill, in the row that best describes it. Then read across to discover what the bird's saying.

What you heard	Did it sound like...	Then it's probably a...	And the yappy bird is...
Too-la-la-la-too!	A relaxed melody?	Song	A songbird looking for love or marking its territory. Common in spring.
	Rhythmic chirps and tweets?	Companion call	Tracking its mate and flock friends.
Awwk!	A sharp, loud call?	Alarm call	Spotting a cat or other predator, alerting companions, and warning off the intruder.
	Loud buzzes and chirps?	Contact call	Traveling in a flock or trying to get another bird's attention.
	Tiny peeps and chirps?	Begging call	A baby bird hungry for breakfast.

Who's That in the Mirror?

You spend a lot of your life in the bathroom. It's a great place to check out your face, but it's also great to learn some truly strange potty science.

Now that you're taking a good look at yourself, what are you, exactly?

Hey! You think you look like this? NOPE! Your face is actually flipped.

Want to see infinity? Reflect a mirror in another mirror.

Pee-yoo! Learn how quickly food goes through your body and out the other end.

Comb your hair—then use that comb to control H_2O and play tricks on your eyes.

Freeze soap bubbles, paint with 'em, or fight 'em against each other!

Brr—why is the floor cold when the towel's warm?

What kind of whirlpool lives in your toilet? Flush to find out.

Unflip Your Face!

Your face in a mirror isn't your real face. It's flipped! Flat mirrors show images that are reversed left to right. Turn yourself around and upside down with this cylindrical mirror.

1. **Grab the mirror sheet** from the opposite page. Find a cardboard bucket (fried-chicken containers work) with a 9-inch (23-cm) diameter. Slice the bucket lengthwise into two curved halves, and snip away the flat bottom part. No bucket? Cut out a 14-inch (35.5-cm) square of posterboard and curve its edges upward into a half-pipe with a 9-inch (23-cm) diameter.

2. **Curve the "mirror"** lengthwise so it forms a half-cylinder. Tape it evenly and smoothly on the inside of one bucket cutout.

3. **Hold the mirror upright,** and then test it: Wink your right eye. Does your reflection wink its right eye? If not, move the mirror farther out until it does. Now your image is no longer reversed: Light bounces off one curved side onto the other and unflips your face. And if you hold the mirror horizontally and move it away from yourself, your image will turn upside down!

A Kid with Kaleidoscope Eyes

Create millions of multiplied reflections with some easy mirror magic.

1. **If you used the mirror sheet** in the experiment above, gently untape it from the cardboard cutout. Smooth it out flat.

2. **Fold the sheet** lengthwise into a long triangular tube—see the diagram at left. Tape its edges together.

3. **Pick something with funky colors:** maybe the tile under your feet, or even the tile pattern on this page. Place one end of the tube near but not smack up against it. Put your eye to the other end, and check out the countless reflections of reflections of reflections.

Want to see *yourself* in a kaleidoscope? Find six 1-by-1-foot (30-by-30-cm) mirror tiles, duct-tape them into an open triangle (two on each side), and put your head inside the triangle. Presto—a zillion yous!

The Goo Inside You

- 1.5% other stuff
- 1% phosphorus
- 1.5% calcium
- 3% nitrogen
- 10% hydrogen
- 18% carbon
- 65% oxygen

You there, in the mirror! Do you ever wonder what, exactly, you're made of? A few chemicals (and buckets of personality) make up your human self.

Check out the graphic at left. You'll notice that a lot of your body is oxygen and hydrogen, in the form of water molecules. You might also wonder what that 1.5 percent "other stuff" consists of: It's a party mix of elements such as zinc, selenium, and cobalt.

But, you argue, "I'm not just a bunch of chemicals. I'm *me!*" You're right—you *are* a unique creature. Read on to find out why.

The Goo That Makes You *You*

To see why you're so special, peek at the gooey DNA in your spit. That's the genetic material found in all your cells, from your nose to your toes—and unless you have an identical twin, no one else in the world has the exact same stuff.

You'll need:
8-ounce (237-mL) measuring cup
Salt
Liquid dish soap
Bowl
Clean cup
Tall, skinny glass jam jar
Plastic wrap
Rubbing alcohol
Plastic straw

1. **Fill the measuring cup** with water and dissolve 1 tablespoon of salt in it.

2. **Mix 1 tablespoon** of liquid dish soap with 3 tablespoons of water in the bowl.

3. **Put 1 teaspoon** of plain water in your mouth. Swish it around and spit it in your clean cup.

4. **Put 1/4 teaspoon** of the salt solution in the jam jar, and then pour that yummy spit water from the cup into the jar.

5. **Add 1/4 teaspoon** of the soap solution to the jar. Tightly cover it with plastic wrap and turn it almost upside down a few times. Be gentle so you don't make bubbles.

6. **Take off the wrap.** Drip 1 teaspoon of rubbing alcohol down the inside of the jar. A white, goopy layer will form on top of the spit-soap-salt potion.

7. **Stick in the straw** to grab some goop. It will be stringy—and those strings are made up of thousands of molecules of your own personal DNA.

8. **Use the magnifier** in this book to check out an extra blob of spit. What do you see in that saliva?

How to Disguise Yourself

How do people recognize that face you see in your mirror every day? They look at its upper part—your eyes, your nose, and especially your hair. Here's an old bank-robber's trick that foils face recognition.

Forget fake glasses or beards. The best disguise? It's a wig! A new hairdo messes with others' memory of your face. Here we put Elvis's hair on three famous people's heads. Who are they? Put a hand over the top, then the bottom, of each face. (Unsure? Answers are at the foot of this page.)

Our brains are designed to detect faces in all kinds of places. →

Two doubled left halves and two doubled right halves of the same woman's face! ←

Science Meets Art: Julian Wolkenstein

Do both sides of your face look the same? No! Each is a bit different, with unique freckles, eye shape, and bone structure. Julian Wolkenstein plays with the idea of *symmetry* (matching sides) by taking an ordinary portrait, splitting it in half, then doubling each half. The result? Two very different images of the same person's face. Try this disorienting trick on your own features. From a computer, print two copies of a picture of your face. Cut one in half vertically. Then flip the image horizontally in photo software, print out that version, and cut it in half vertically. Tape one flipped left side to one normal right side. Then attach one flipped right side to one normal left side. Compare both new pictures to the regular photo of yourself. Wow! Who knew you were a kid of so many faces?

Conjure with Combs

Tame your bedhead, and then put that comb to wilder use by creating eye-dazzling patterns.

1 **Find two combs,** and hold one right in front of the other at an angle.

3 **Slide the combs** side to side and watch the moiré pattern move. Rotate one comb and hold the other still—how does the pattern change?

2 **Look through the teeth—** a pattern of light and dark shows up. That's called a *moiré* pattern, and it appears where two repetitive patterns of lines, circles, or dots imperfectly overlap. The cool thing about moiré is that it's not formed by the objects, but by your eyes as they add the two images together.

Once you're a pro moiré spotter, you'll see the patterns everywhere. Look through two chain-link fences on the schoolyard, or fold a thin, fine scarf and hold it to the light, moving the fabric around to watch the patterns dance. Moiré magnifies differences between repetitive patterns. If two patterns are exactly lined up, you get zero moiré. The tiniest misalignment, though, and voilà—big-time moiré. And as misalignment increases, moiré lines look thinner and closer together.

Why Does the Floor Feel Cold When the Towel Feels Warm?

Your bare tootsies freeze on the bathroom tiles in the morning, but your face towel feels warm. Why the difference? Our hands are lousy judges of true temperature.

1 Put your palm on the towel, the glass, the towel rod, and the floor in turn. Is each surface warm or cold? Write down the objects, ranking them by how warm they feel.

2 Wait a few minutes, then slap the thermo strip on each surface. You'll notice something freaky: They're all about the same temperature. Why? Some, like the metal towel rod and tiles, are good heat conductors. They rapidly sap heat from your hand, so your nerves sense them as cold. Others, such as the towel, are poor heat conductors. They don't suck away your hand's heat, and so they seem warm.

Static Magic

Yo, Superman, try this: Bend the flow of rushing water with nothing but a comb and your own hair!

Give your head a really thorough combing until your hair crackles. Turn the sink faucet to low or medium flow, hold the comb nearby, and watch the water warp toward the comb.

What's the Deal?

Everything in the universe is made up of atoms, which are composed of three kinds of charged particles: *protons* (with a positive charge), *electrons* (negative charge), and *neutrons* (neutral charge). As you comb your hair, you pull electrons away from it and negatively charge the comb. Water molecules have negatively and positively charged ends, so the negatively charged comb draws the water molecules' positive ends toward the comb. Opposites *do* attract!

The Scoop on Poop

What goes in must come out—it's a law of nature, or at least a law of our tummies. But what *is* poop, anyway?

Let's say you have a delicious feast of corn on the cob. It travels from your mouth down your throat and into your stomach and intestines, which break down the corn and pull out nutrients to fuel your body.

But there's stuff left over: fibrous material; extra water, protein, fats, and salts; bacteria released by your liver and intestines; and *bilirubin*, worn-out blood cells that your body tosses in its trash chute.

Wanna stage a poop race? (Sure you do!) Find your winner with a poop journal, plus a few slow-digesting—but super-nourishing—foods.

Food	Time you ate it	Time it showed up	What do you see?
Dark-green kale (Look for greenish poop.)			
Red beets (Usually shows up as red poop!)			
Green snap peas (Watch for little green fragments.)			
Add your favorite food here!			

The Asparagus Aroma

If nature calls soon after you munch asparagus, you might notice a certain...scent. Some people say it smells like flowers. Others say it just smells funky. Still others smell nothing at all.

When we eat asparagus, our bodies quickly metabolize its ammonia- and sulfur-containing compounds—that's the stinky stuff. (Young asparagus holds higher levels of these compounds.) As for people who say they can't smell asparagus pee? They're telling the truth: Scientists say only a quarter of the population can sniff it out.

Which Way Do the Toilets Go?

Popular wisdom says that toilets in the Northern Hemisphere swirl water counterclockwise and those in the Southern Hemisphere swoosh it clockwise. But you can flush that story right down the pot.

Before we talk toilets, let's talk space. The Earth is a ball, and a line called the equator wraps around it at its widest point. As the Earth spins, any point on the equator spins faster than one north or south of that line. This twists masses of air and seawater counterclockwise in the Northern Hemisphere and the opposite way in the Southern.

Some people argue that the same force affects tiny water bodies, like those in toilets. But water drains out of a toilet in a direction set by the pot itself: whether it jets or swirls water into the bowl, and whether water passes over bumpy surfaces as it's flushed away.

Round and 'round it goes, but which way it spins, nobody knows...

Birds Do It, Bees Do It . . .

Scientists can tell all sorts of things about animals and people—alive or dead—by poking through their poop, including what they ate and when they lived. Take a peek at some of their samples.

Deer poop out little pellets of mashed-up plant fiber.

Elephant dung is big and straw-filled...and it doesn't stink.

Stringy goldfish poop is full of worm and bug bits and sticks to the fish for a while.

Owl feces are tidy little packages of indigestible rodent fur and bones.

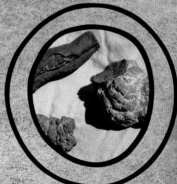

Fossilized dino poop helps scientists figure out whether the creature ate meat or plants.

Bubble-o-Rama

They float and bob—but they're no lightweights. Discover the wonder of bubble land with these games.

Brew Up Bubble Juice

Fragile little bubbles are so yesterday. So stir up some wicked potion for ultra-strong bubbles—just mix ⅔ cup (158 mL) of dish soap, 2 tablespoons of glycerin (buy it at a drugstore), and 1 gallon (3.8 L) of water in a bucket, and you've got mighty bubble juice.

Blobjets d'Art

Preserve your beautiful bubbles by turning them into art. Put ½ cup (118 mL) of bubble juice in a jar, and then add three more squirts of dish soap for super-foaminess. Mix in a few blasts of tempera paint. Stir, pour the glop in a pie tin, and wet a straw. (Anything that touches bubbles must be wet. Dry stuff = bubble death.) Blow, baby, blow until bubbles fill the tin. Touch an uncoated sheet of paper to the bubbles and set it aside. Which shapes and angles do you see on the paper—triangles, circles, squares? When the paper's dry, pick a new paint color and press a new bubble print over the first.

Bubble Brrr! 🔍

How to extend a bubble's life? Freeze it! Fill the end of a wet straw with bubble juice and blow some big ones over a wet plate. When a nice, round specimen floats down, gently set the plate flat in the freezer. After an hour (you can peek from time to time), lift the plate out of the fridge. Ice "flowers" will spangle the bubble before it deflates and dies. Check 'em out with the magnifier in this book.

Bubble Battle

Pour bubble juice on a cookie sheet, dip two plastic straws in water, and give one to your sister. Now declare war! Who can blow the biggest dome, or one dome inside another? Can you corner her bubbles with your battalion of mighty bubble warriors? Then make peace, stick your straws next to each other, and build a tower of bubbles together. How high can you go before its "bricks" burst?

Hair Dryer Gravity Defier

Before you work your look, work your dryer to defeat gravity.

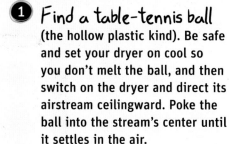

1 Find a table-tennis ball (the hollow plastic kind). Be safe and set your dryer on cool so you don't melt the ball, and then switch on the dryer and direct its airstream ceilingward. Poke the ball into the stream's center until it settles in the air.

2 Move into a corner, where the airstream will blow the ball far higher. Now grab the ball and slowly pull it outward—you'll feel the airstream sucking it back. Let go of the ball, and it will bobble, wobble, and finally return to its original float.

Serenade Your Shower

If you rock out while you scrub down, you're not alone—most folks' voices sound sweet under the spray. You're surrounded by hard tile or plastic that bounces your voice back to your ears, amplifying it. As your song ricochets, some sound waves stretch out, which adds richness to their tone. And the water's roar dampens your missed notes and misjudged arias. So warble away!

What's the Deal?

This experiment isn't really about hairdryers. In fact, it shows you how airplanes fly! When the ball is in the blower's blast, air hits its bottom and slows, making a high-pressure region on which the ball rests. In a corner, the compressed airstream lofts the ball still higher. When you pull the ball outward, air rushes around its curved surface, leaving an area of low pressure. Normal atmospheric pressure pushes the ball back into the airstream. Airplane wings operate in a similar way: Their wings, curved on top, force air downward. And as Isaac Newton figured out, for every action there's an equal and opposite reaction, so air under the wings lifts them, and the plane zips along.

Time for Pants

Yes, even your closet is a laboratory! Dig through those heaps of clothes and you'll find a whole realm of textures, senses, and sounds to investigate.

Pop quiz! How much of your life do you spend getting dressed?

Your shoes can sing sweet music— just pull out a lace to hear it!

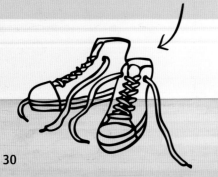

In these drawers is a super-strong electricity generator called... your sweater.

The Secret World of Fabric 🔍

Before you don your duds, get up close to find out how your clothes really look and feel.

1 *Run a touch test:* Pick a few favorite pieces of clothing, shut your eyes, and put your fingers on each in turn. Keep still for 30 seconds. What do you feel? Unless you wiggle your fingers, after your initial "That's wool!" reaction, you can't tell one surface from the next. Your fingertips' nerves just stop firing.

2 *Snag the magnifier* from this book and peer at the fabric in the closet at left. Does the corduroy look smooth or like rows in a field? Is the denim blue or a blob of multicolored dots? Under an even stronger magnifier, you'd also see all the empty space inside cloth—and everything else we think is solid.

Cotton fibers

Under a high-powered microscope, cotton's fibers are long, flat, ribbony tubes. (Smooth, glassy rods mean a fabric is likely polyester.)

Wool fibers

Sheep hair—better known as wool—look barbed under a microscope. When they're heated, as in a dryer, the barbs grab one another, and your sweater turns from fluffy into flattened felt.

Cotton terry-cloth towel

Cotton bedsheet

Polyester carpet fiber

Polyester fleece fiber

Ants in Your Pants

You've got a brand-new pair of jeans to wear today! Slip them on, admire yourself, and—uh-oh. The tag is driving you nuts. You've got a bad case of *formication:* the creepy-crawly feeling (named for *formica,* "ant" in Latin) that arises when tiny hairs on your skin sense that something unfamiliar is bending or flattening them. To de-formicate, you can clip the tag, scratch your butt all day, or be patient: The itch fades as the teeny nerves at the base of the hairs stop freaking out and accept the feeling as normal.

Dance with Your Sweater

Use your wardrobe to amp up some electric boogaloo.

1 **Lay out** an 11-by-17-inch (28-by-43-cm) sheet of paper on your desk, and arrange four tuna cans on it, one in each corner.

2 **Scatter a couple handfuls** of crumbled polystyrene foam in the square made by the cans.

3 **Now you need** a thick square of clear plastic, the same size as the paper. Rest it evenly on the cans.

4 **Pull a fuzzy wool sweater** out of your dresser and rub the plastic hard with it. Now watch as the foam crumbs dance and shimmy from paper to plastic and back again.

What's the Deal?

The plastic sheet and the foam pieces start out electrically neutral—they have an equal number of positive and negative charges. When you rub the sweater on the sheet, its wool transfers negative charges to the plastic. These negative charges polarize the bits of foam, attracting positive charges to their tops and pushing negative charges to their bottoms. The attraction between the negative plastic and the positive charge on the foam pieces' tops makes the pieces leap to the plastic. When a bit of foam hits the plastic, some of the plastic's negative charge flows to the foam, and its top becomes electrically neutral. But since the whole piece of foam was originally neutral, it now has excess negative charge. The negatively charged foam and the negatively charged plastic repel each other, so the foam boings back to the table. The piece's excess negative charge drains into the table, so the foam becomes neutral—and ready to jump up to the plastic again!

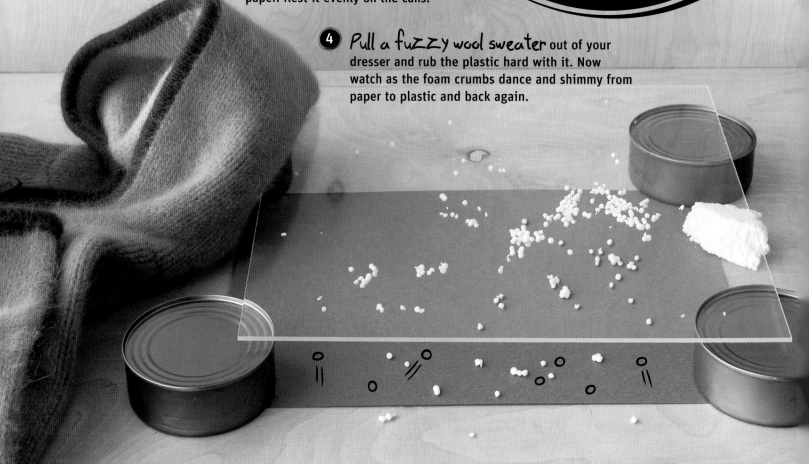

The Tiny Pants Challenge

Use a simple trick of perspective to dress your friends in teeny-tiny clothes.

① **Draw a pair of pants** (the sillier, the better!). Cut them out, glue them on card stock, and trim around them.

② **Carry the pants** with you as you go through the day.

③ **When you meet a friend,** tell her to stand several paces away from you. Then hold the pants in front of yourself and close one eye. This messes up your depth perception, and suddenly your goofy minipants fit your large-as-life pal.

Ping!

Harmonies in Your Head

You've watched Westerns in which outlaws squash their ears to the dirt to listen for the posse's hoofbeats. Try a similar trick to make melodious tunes only you can hear—using a shoestring instead of a desert road.

❶ **Wrap a 3-foot- (1-m-) long shoestring** behind your head. Pull the string ends forward, right over your ear holes, and hold them together in front of your face.

❷ **Pluck the shoestring** and listen to its tone. Pull the string tighter or loosen it to make its pitch higher or lower.

❸ **The cool thing?** The vibration that creates the sound travels along the shoestring, vibrates your skull, and gets directly into your ears. But it doesn't have enough energy to enter the ears of anyone else nearby.

The Breakfast Lab

Juice, cereal, eggs, and tea: They're all part of a tasty breakfast. And they're all subjects for very tasty science tests.

Spin your teacup around to see cosmic forces at work.

You're crunching a mouthful of metal every morning in these flakes!

Squish, squash, and slice to learn about fruit guts.

Turn white milk into an awesome rainbow!

Water: It can cut like a sword. Or fake it really well.

You can scramble these eggs, but it's more fun to experiment on them.

The Juice-Tasting Challenge

Tummy's rumbling—it's time to eat! Did you know that you "eat" with your nose and eyes as well as your mouth? It's true. Put your family's sniffers and peepers to the test with this juice-guessing game.

You'll need:
Masking tape
4 glasses
Pen and paper
4 flavors of juice
A partner (a brother or sister will do)
4 food colorings

1 Stick a piece of tape on the bottom of each glass and number them one to four, making sure your partner can't see the numbers. Pour one type of juice into each glass.

2 Send your partner out of the room. Drip a different food coloring into each juice and stir so your partner can't recognize the juice by its color alone. Record the number, juice type, and color in each glass on a piece of paper.

What's the Deal?

You've just learned something amazing: Your nose has a secret superpower. It "tastes" more flavor than your tongue does. In fact, its smell receptors are ten thousand times more sensitive than your taste buds, and they also can tell you a lot more about food and drink than your eyes can. Your partner probably couldn't accurately guess the juice flavor with her eyes or tongue alone, but her nose knew the real score!

3 Call your partner back. Tell her to hold her nose, sip from each glass, and guess the juice. If she's like most people, she'll be kind of confused—her eyes and tongue give her two conflicting flavor messages.

4 Ask her to unplug her nose, close her eyes, and sniff the juice before drinking it. Her guesses should be on target now. All hail the mighty schnoz!

Got a Genius Tongue? 🔍

Some people don't just taste—they *super-taste*. Flavors are incredibly intense for these rare-tongued people. Have a super-taster in your family? A dribble of blue food coloring will reveal the truth.

1 **Write down everyone's name.** Then ask your first volunteer to dry his tongue with a paper towel.

2 **Drip blue food coloring** on a swab and paint the tip of his tongue. Tell him to swish saliva around his tongue and swallow until his whole tongue is beautifully blue.

3 **Stick a reinforcement circle** on his tongue tip. Ask someone to hold the flashlight while you use the magnifier to look at the tongue area in that circle. Pretty pink bumps—*papillae*, which hold taste buds—show up against the blue.

4 **Count up** the papillae you see. Write that number by his name. Now call up the next volunteer and repeat. (Even pets are fair game, if they'll hold still.)

You'll need:
Everybody in the house!
Pencil and paper
Paper towels
Blue food coloring
Cotton swabs
Reinforcements (the circles you paste around binder-paper holes)
Flashlight
Magnifier from this book

What's the Deal?
Papillae each hold up to 15 taste buds. The more you've got, the more you taste. Super-tasters have more than 30 papillae in the reinforcement-circle area. They often love sweets but hate bitter things like coffee. But about half of us have only 10 to 30 papillae in the area. We're just called tasters (yawn). And the rest—nontasters who detect flavor but aren't picky—sport fewer than 10. Ask your family if they like bitter foods. Do the super-tasters say no?

Slice a Straw with Water

Did you know H$_2$O's as sharp as a sword? It's not really, but when you drop a straw into a glassful, water sure *looks* wicked sharp.

Fill a clear glass, plop in a straw, and let it rest against the rim. Get eye level with the glass. The straw's in one piece—so why does it appear as if it's cut in two?

The reason: The water bends the light coming from the straw's sunken section, so that part shifts slightly in your vision. But light coming from the section of the straw that's above the water doesn't bend on its way to your eyes.

The Big Eggshell Breakdown

Eggs are amazing. Baby birds hatch out of them, they taste great, and—as you'll see here—they're perfect for kitchen-counter chemistry experiments.

① **Stick an egg in a cup,** and then pour in enough white vinegar to completely cover it. See teeny bubbles forming on the shell? That's carbon dioxide, and it's produced when acidic vinegar hits the calcium of the shell.

② **Cover the cup** with plastic wrap and leave it alone for 24 hours. The next morning, ladle out the egg with a spoon. The shell is now dissolving away. Dump out the old vinegar and cover the squashy egg with fresh vinegar. Then put plastic wrap on the cup and let it sit for another 24 hours.

③ **On the third morning,** carefully spoon out the egg and rinse it under the tap. The shell should be totally gone now! As you can see in this picture, just an alien-looking blob of egg white and yolk remains, held inside a thin membrane.

Keep playing! Put the naked egg in a cup of water. It swells because more water is in the cup than in the egg, so water seeps into the egg membrane. Then plop the egg in a cup of corn syrup (made of water and sugar). Now there's more water *in* the egg than outside. The egg's water leaches out, and it collapses like a sad balloon.

Fruit Salad Surprise

Before you get your morning fruit into your tummy, get your fingers into the fruit to explore the wild varieties of fruit peels, pulp, juice, and seeds. Can't find these exotics in the store? Squish and squash oranges, blueberries, or other available stuff!

Noni
(Southeast Asia)

Passion fruit
(South America)

Both of these fruits hold their crunchy seeds and sweet juice in panels of tiny sacs called *arils*. Halve the fruits, bang the halves on a bowl edge, then spoon out and munch the gemlike little arils.

Pomegranate
(Mediterranean)

Some fruit protects itself with cactusy thorns, tough skin, and ultra-tangy flesh. Don't be scared: Just peel these guys, slice 'em in half, and chew 'em seeds and all. Pucker up!

Prickly pear
(Central America)

Mangosteen (Indonesia)

Durian (Thailand)

These fruits hide their bizarre insides behind spiny skin. Durian has big, yolklike pods of sweet but rank-smelling flesh. Rambutan boasts both a huge, eyeball-shaped central seed and a layer of flesh that you can nibble away from it.

Giant seeds and teeny seeds: Fruit flaunts both styles. Mangosteen has giant white seeds that you fork out to eat and bitter pulp that you toss. Dragon fruit has zillions of seeds peppered through it, and you can run a spoon around the flesh to free it from the scaly rind.

Rambutan (Malaysia)

Dragon fruit (Asia and the Americas)

The Rainbow Explosion

Morning milk too boring and bland? Blast in some rainbows!

1 *Pour about* ½ *inch* (1.25 cm) of whole or 2 percent milk into a saucer. Let it come to room temperature.

2 *Plop several drops* of different food coloring onto the milk's surface. They might spread a little, but they'll stay where you put them.

3 *Soak the end* of a cotton swab in rubbing alcohol. Touch it to the color drops, which will explode into wild whorls and bursts.

Set up another dish of milk, with colored drops near the center, to stage a color drop derby. Dip the end of a toothpick in dish soap and then poke the pick end into the middle of the dish. The bright blobs will race for the edges as if their lives depended on it.

What's the Deal?

Water—and food coloring, which is mostly water—hangs together in droplets because water molecules are attracted to one another (it's sorta sweet). This is called *surface tension*. Milk, which also is mostly water, has this property, too. When you add rubbing alcohol (or soap), its molecules push apart the water molecules. Surface tension breaks down most at the spots where you put the alcohol, so water molecules elsewhere in the saucer pull water molecules away from milk near the alcohol. The food coloring swirls as all these molecules dance.

Spin Your Teacup

Investigate awesome physical forces
at work in your daily cup of tea.

Fill a teacup with water and loose-leaf tea. (Dislike
tea? You can also try this with water and confetti.)
Let the tea cool, then set it on a smooth surface, like a
counter, and whirl it by its handle. Notice how the leaves
spin to the cup's edges, and, if you peer in, you'll see that
the water becomes deeper at the edges than it is in the cup's
center. This is because the spinning water is being pushed against
the cup's sides. Now stop the cup—the liquid keeps rotating, but now
it falls from the cup's sides and drags the leaves into a central heap.

Magnetize Your Munch

There's iron in that cereal of yours. Dig
it out with nifty magnetic magic.

1 Pour a serving of cereal
on the plate. Use your fingers to crush
it into tiny crumbs, then smooth the
crumbs into a thin layer.

2 Hover your magnet right
over—but don't touch—the crumbs.
Do any move? If not, smoosh them
more. (Use the bottom of the water
glass to crush crumbs extra-fine.)
Wipe the paper towel across the
magnet. Do see fine black grains
on the towel? You've pulled out
some iron!

You'll need:

Iron-fortified cereal*

China plate

An ultra-strong magnet,
such as a rare-earth one

Water glass

Paper towel

Zip-top plastic bag

Water

* Check the label to ensure it contains at least
18 mg of iron per serving. (Iron in our food
keeps our red blood cells happy.)

3 Now mine for iron with water. Crush another serving
and put it in the zip-top bag. Fill the bag with water and seal
it. Touch the magnet to the bag to see if a few black grains will
drift toward the bag's plastic side. Then empty your plate, pour
a layer of water on it, and float a few whole flakes. Can you
steer them like little boats by holding the magnet above them?

4 Pick the flakes out of the water. Finely crush
another serving of cereal and sprinkle it on the
water. Can you make out tiny black specks? Use the
magnet to steer those guys to one side of the plate.
You might collect quite a clump—just look at all the
metal you're munching every morning!

The Street Underneath Your Feet

Sneak a peek downward when you walk down your street in the morning—that plain old gray sidewalk under your sneakers is a lot cooler than you might think.

They won't break your mama's back, but cracks do hold a lot of secrets. What makes them? Do they follow special patterns?

Are these feet? No, they're rulers! Use 'em to measure the distance you walk.

We pretty much ignore our shadows, but guess what? They can show you how the Earth spins and orbits around the Sun.

Gobble up some cookies—then stage a downhill race with their tins.

There's lots to discover when you take a crayon and paper to the ground to make rubbings!

The Downtown Rubdown

Find out your hometown's secrets by making a street rubbing. All you need is a few crayons and sturdy paper—plus your own curious eyes.

❶ *Nearly anything's fair game* for a rubbing (but avoid graveyards and private property). Look for fancy manhole covers, building friezes, contractors' plaques set in sidewalks, and funky gratings. Or try your first rubbing on the sidewalk "shapes" at left: animals and leaves often make prints in wet concrete, and they're perfect rubbing material once the sidewalk's dry.

❷ *Dry and brush dust* off the object. Hold or tape a sheet of paper on your target, peel the jacket off a crayon, and rub its side over the paper until texture appears.

❸ *Watch as the image deepens.* See anything you didn't expect or don't recognize? An unknown street name, an unexplained date? Look it up! Rubbings can reveal lost or forgotten parts of a city's history.

Give your shadow four arms or handmade antlers!

Play with Your Shadow

That gray thing called your shadow doesn't just drag along after your feet. Get to know it by making it do silly tricks for you.

Try a sidewalk shadow show: Collect a few friends at your back and get everyone to turn away from the Sun. Stick out your arms and wave them up and down—hey, you're a lizard!

Now find a blank wall, put your hands on top of your head with your elbows out, and stand by a friend. Scrunch your necks down into your shoulders to make monster eyeball shadows.

Only round wheels roll, right? Think again. Square wheels can race along, too.

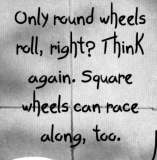

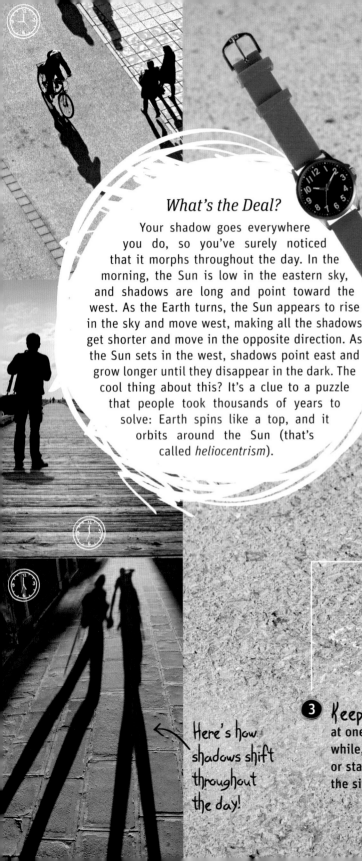

The Rad Shadow Sketch

Scared of your own shadow? Then grab a favorite toy and turn its shadow into art that illustrates an ancient solar-system secret.

What's the Deal?

Your shadow goes everywhere you do, so you've surely noticed that it morphs throughout the day. In the morning, the Sun is low in the eastern sky, and shadows are long and point toward the west. As the Earth turns, the Sun appears to rise in the sky and move west, making all the shadows get shorter and move in the opposite direction. As the Sun sets in the west, shadows point east and grow longer until they disappear in the dark. The cool thing about this? It's a clue to a puzzle that people took thousands of years to solve: Earth spins like a top, and it orbits around the Sun (that's called *heliocentrism*).

1 Outline your toy's shadow with chalk.

2 Wait an hour and outline its shadow with a new color of chalk. Did the shadow get longer? Shorter? Is it squashed or more defined?

3 Keep tracing the shadow at one-hour intervals. After a while, you'll have a colorful fan or starburst shape of shadows on the sidewalk.

Here's how shadows shift throughout the day!

No time for a daylong sketch? No worries. Choose a tall object such as a lamp post, whose shadow changes more dramatically at shorter intervals. You can sketch it every 20 minutes.

That's the Way the Sidewalk Crumbles

Bet you always thought sidewalks crack however they want to. In fact, they fall apart in pretty orderly ways.

1 First find your crack. Primo hunting spots: empty sidewalks and playgrounds where signs, manhole covers, or roots shatter pavement.

2 Grab a protractor— the plastic semicircle that you use in geometry class. Put it on the concrete and measure angles between the cracks.

What's the Deal?

Are you finding many 90- and 120-degree angles? The 90-degree ones are caused by stuff stuck into the sidewalk, which exerts unequal stress on the concrete and splits it in angles perpendicular to the object breaking it. The trios of cracks separated by the 120-degree angles form under uniform stress from temperature swings, upwelling water, or shifting dirt underneath the sidewalk.

Even volcanoes suffer stress! If you ever visit an old lava bed, look for cracks. As hot lava cools, it shrinks and splits. Cracks meeting at 120-degree angles are the shortest ones that can relieve stress—and nature often takes the shortest path and uses the least amount of energy to do its job.

Science Meets Art: Andy Goldsworthy

Andy Goldsworthy makes his artwork out of the randomness of nature. For *Carefully Broken Pebbles* (1985), the artist snapped oval stones in half, scraped their edges white, and then arranged them in a vanishing spiral. In other works, he uses natural materials such as leaves, flowers, branches, and even ice.

If stone-cracking appeals to you, find a few large rocks, wrap them in a blanket, borrow a hammer, and tap— softly, then hard—to watch fascinating fissures appear. Photograph pleasing patterns, and keep smacking! Set the fragments into patterns, or just observe what occurs as solid matter crumbles apart.

Race Along on Square Wheels

Everyone knows you can't put a square peg in a round hole. But you *can* make a square wheel zip along a round road!

1 Hot-glue the toilet-paper rolls onto the foam-core rectangle. Make sure they touch each other. This is your road!

2 Cut out a 2-by-5-inch (5-by-13-cm) posterboard piece for the car's body. Then snip two drinking straws into 2-inch (5-cm) sections and hot-glue them 3/8 inch (9.5 cm) from either end of the car body's underside.

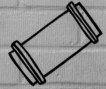

3 Cut four square wheels with 2-inch (5-cm) sides out of posterboard. Pencil an X from corner to corner to find each wheel's center, and poke a hole there with a thumbtack.

4 To make axles, cut the bamboo skewers into two 5-inch (13-cm) pieces. Slide a wheel on a skewer so it's 3/4 inch (2 cm) from the unpointed end, then slip the skewer through one straw. Slide on the second wheel. Then do the same with the second skewer-and-wheel pair.

5 Poke a hole in one end of the car between the edge and straw. Stick one end of a paper clip in the hole. Loop a length of string through the paper clip.

You'll need:
Glue gun
24 empty toilet-paper rolls
4-by-30-inch (10-by-76-cm) foam-core slab
Scissors
Posterboard
2 drinking straws
Pencil
Thumbtack
2 bamboo skewers
Paper clip
String

6 It's race time! Put your car on the "road" and pull the string. It'll roll nearly as gracefully as any round-wheeled hot rod does.

Create a Stride Ruler

Long ago, people measured length in all sorts of funky units—barleycorns, ells, rods. Most fell out of style, but you can invent a unique unit using your own two feet.

On your next stroll, carry a ruler and chalk. Draw a start line on the sidewalk and put your toes right behind that line. Take 10 normal steps; when you finish, chalk a line next to your toe.

Measure the distance you cover start to finish. Divide that number by 10 to get each stride's length. Note: *Stride* length is the distance from one heel's strike to the next strike of the same heel. *Step* length is the distance from one heel's strike to the strike of the opposite heel.

Use your stride length to measure distance. If you count off 1,500 strides to school and each one is 30 inches (76 cm) long, the trip is 45,000 inches, or 3,750 feet (1,143 m), long.

The Colossal Cookie-Tin Race

Can wheels of the same size race downhill at different speeds? Sure can. To find out why, round up a friend—and a whole bunch of cookies.

1 Devour all the cookies from two round tins of the same size, with your pal's help. (And don't tell your mom.)

2 At a hardware store, buy adhesive-backed Velcro and 10 metal washers, each weighing ¼ pound (0.1 kg).

3 Stick five washers evenly around the bottom of one tin with Velcro. In the middle of the other tin, stack five washers, using Velcro between each to hold them down. Close the lids on the tins.

4 Find a steep street with an even sidewalk. Each of you grabs a tin and rolls it downhill on edge. Which one reaches the base of the hill first?

What's the Deal?

The tin with the washers in its middle always wins. Both tins, at the top of the hill, have identical *potential energy*—they're at the same height and they have identical mass. But that mass is differently distributed between the tins. The tin that has the washers around its edges uses up more potential energy just to get rolling. The tin with its mass at its center saves its energy for the downhill run.

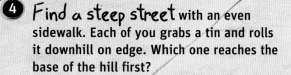

LAB #06

The Science of School

Writing, reading, 'rithmetic—the classroom is where you really train that brain. Give it extra exercise with some rad schoolday science games.

Psych out your brain with a fake memory game.

Tummy rumbling? Eat a sentence salad!

Build a leaning tower of textbooks.

Can you twirl like a skater using only a chair?

Make infinite loops and shapes out of paper!

Words Versus Colors

Confuse the class with a game that pits their ability to ID colors against their skill at reading words.

1 Round up a rainbow of dry-erase markers. On the whiteboard on the facing page, draw a table with three columns and six rows.

2 Write the word *red* in one table box in blue marker. Write *green* in another box in a different color, and *brown* in another box, again in a new color. Don't put words in the same color next to each other, and don't write color names in their actual colors.

3 Go wild with more markers: Write *pink* in green marker, *black* in red, and so on until the table's full of color names written in the wrong colors.

4 Ask a friend to read each word out loud. Time him on your watch. Then time him again as he says the color each word's written in—he'll splutter because his eyes pick up the colors but his brain registers the words.

Make a new table of colored words, flip the whiteboard upside down, and ask your friend to name the colors that the words are written in. He'll zip through them now—his brain ignores the flipped words, which are hard to read, in favor of the hues.

Pleasingly Peculiar Pictures

Tape. Dry-erase pens. Sticky notes. A few classmates and the whiteboard on the opposite page. That's all you need for a rip-roaring game called Exquisite Corpse.

1 Make up a theme for a picture: monsters, houses, whatever you like.

2 The first player puts a sticky note on the whiteboard. Then she lifts it, draws the top of the picture (making sure the others can't see it), and lowers the note. A bit of the drawing should peek out to prompt the next player's work.

3 One by one, each person puts a new sticky below the last, then draws a new section of the picture without peeking at the others. Everyone leaves a bit of their drawing sticking out.

4 When everyone has added to the Corpse, rip off all the stickies to see your artwork. It might look random; it might be gorgeous. But it *will* be the funniest dead guy in town.

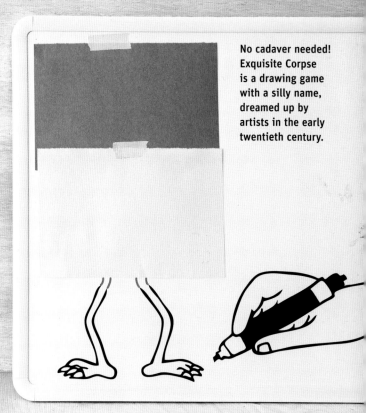

No cadaver needed! Exquisite Corpse is a drawing game with a silly name, dreamed up by artists in the early twentieth century.

The Dizzying Desk Chair Demo

Show your classmates how to morph into a momentum machine using only a chair, two books, and a pal.

What's the Deal?

This brief game reveals a major law of physics: *angular momentum*, which tells you how hard it'll be to stop or start a spinning object—the larger the angular momentum, the harder it will be to stop the object or get it going. Angular momentum is the product of *angular velocity* (how many degrees in a circle you spin each second), your *mass*, and how far your mass is from the spin's center. If one of these factors changes, so does another to keep overall momentum the same. So, when you bring in your arms during a twirlathon, the distance from the spin's center to your arms' mass shortens. That smaller radius increases your rate of rotation, because the overall angular momentum must stay the same. And the books load your hands with more mass, so you spin faster still.

1 **Find a chair** that spins very easily (ask politely and maybe your teacher will let you borrow his). Sit on it with a heavy book in each hand and hold them outward, away from your body.

2 **Now ask a classmate** to spin you around. Once you're whirling at a good speed, tell her to step back. Pull your arms, and the books, in toward your body. Yeehaw—you spin even faster!

Stack It Up

Defy gravity with this curving, tilting tower of books.

1 **With your teacher's okay,** ask your friends for their copies of the class textbook. (The books must be identical or the trick will fall flat!)

2 **Stack the books** so all the spines face you and the pile is even. Push the top book as far right as it can go without falling.

3 **Leave the top book alone,** and slide the one below it as far right as it can go without it or the top one falling. Every time you shift a book, you find a new center of gravity for it and the books over it. Each book edge is a *fulcrum* (supporting point) that bears the weight of the books above it.

4 **Work your way down,** shifting books rightward as you go. A formula explains this game: You can move the top book one-half of the second book's length, the second and third books one-quarter the length of the books below them, and so on. But if you move lower books as far as upper ones: *timber!*

Make a Fake Memory

You can trust your own memories...or *can* you?

1 *Pass this book to a friend* and have her slowly read this word list to you.

tasty
honey
berry
heart

nice
sugar
chocolate
candy

tart
soda
good
pie

2 *Take three minutes* to write down all the words you remember. (No peeking.) You'll get most words correct. But you might also include a related one, such as *sweet,* that's not in the actual list. Why? Your *associative memory* tricked you! When you think about one thing (sugary treats), you think about related things (sweetness). And that association can be so strong that it creates a false memory.

3 *Now write down your own list of words* and try this test on your friend. Select words that all relate to a theme, such as an emotion, an activity, or a quality (speed, darkness, or fun, for example). Read the words to her and ask her to write them down. Does her list contain associative-memory bloopers, too?

Shake Up a Sentence Salad

You can't eat it, but a sentence salad is a great goofy way to figure out why words fit—and don't fit—together.

1 *Find five sheets of construction paper:* yellow, green, red, purple, and blue. Cut each into eight strips.

2 *On each side of the yellow pieces,* write a noun (such as *apple*). Put adjectives (such as *hot*) on the green pieces, verbs (such as *run*) on red ones. Prepositions *(over, under)* go on purple ones, conjunctions *(and, or)* on blue. Don't repeat any words.

3 *Salad-shakin' time!* Heap your 80 tasty words into a box and bounce them around.

4 *Pull out eight strips in this order:* green, yellow, red, purple, green, yellow, blue, red. Line them up and then read your salad.

What's the Deal?

Before we explain, flip over the strips in your salad and read the words you wrote on the other side. You'll still see a real sentence because the parts of speech and their order remain the same. "Big Pig Jumps over Old Log and Laughs" and "Blue House Falls into Sad Lake but Dances" both run adjective, noun, verb, preposition, adjective, noun, conjunction, verb. Though you might not know all the rules of grammar, the salad proves that you do know *syntax*—or how words fit together. You've absorbed syntax all your life, so you can recognize what is and what is not a sentence—even if you can't tell a conjunction from a cupcake.

The Math Around You 🔍

Math's not just in books. It's in plants and buildings and your very own body—all of which follow surprisingly precise mathematical patterns. Search these patterns out during your schoolday.

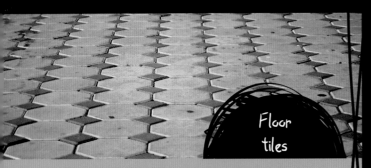

Floor tiles

In the tiles and mosaics of school walls and halls, you'll spot *tessellations*—patterns of repeating geometric shapes laid edge to edge without space between them. The shapes can be identical or different. A *tangram,* too, uses pieces with edge-to-edge spacing in a puzzle that you can arrange into a square or near-infinite other pictures.

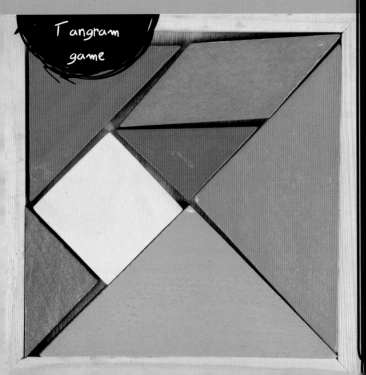

Tangram game

Gym architecture

Symmetry is an inescapable math principle—our brains love balanced, proportional arrangements, so we use them everywhere in our buildings. Look around school to spot symmetrical walls, windows, and other architectural features. Their identical elements often seem to converge, along lines called *orthogonals,* at a distant vanishing point.

Auditorium seats

Romanesco broccoli

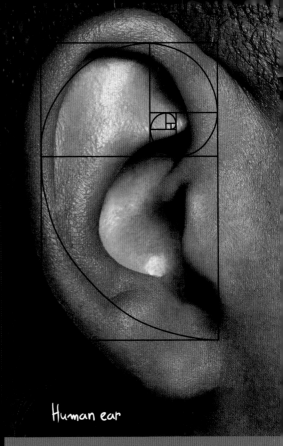

Human ear

Fractal patterns are branching, ever-smaller repetitions of the same shapes. They lurk in your school lunch (romanesco broccoli shows them off well) and even inside your body, in your nerves, lungs, and veins. In fact, you're reading about fractals right now by using the fractal-patterned nerves below: these are the nerves of your eye!

The funky pattern known as the *golden ratio* (in which smaller rectangles in a diminishing spiral are proportional to larger ones) shows up in everything from new ferns to seashells to the curves of our own ears.

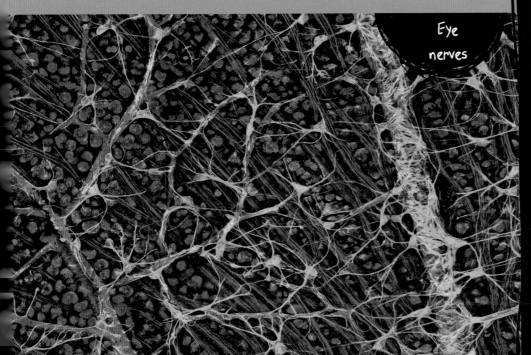

Eye nerves

Fossilized nautilus

53

Twist Your Brain with a Mobius Band

Paper's an ordinary thing—you read it, you blow your nose in it—that can perform freaky physical tricks. It can even transform from a two-sided object into a single-sided one.

1. **Cut a 1-inch- (2.5-cm-) wide strip** from a sheet of paper. Stick a piece of clear tape on one end.

2. **Make a loop:** Bring the taped and untaped ends of the paper together, as if you were going to make a circular band. But before you tape the ends together, flip the untaped end over, and then attach the taped end to it. Now you have a twisted Mobius band.

3. **Pencil an X** on the band's middle. Draw a line from the X all the way around the band and back to the X. You'll see that you never pick up your pencil the whole time you're drawing. That's because a Mobius band has only one side—though it sure *looks* like it has two.

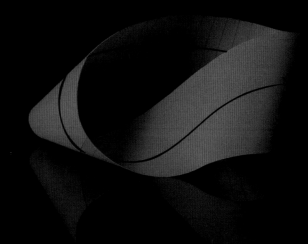

The Exponential Paper Fold

Bet your milk money on this paper-folding trick, and we guarantee you'll have more dairy than you can drink.

1. **Spread out a sheet of newspaper.** Ask a friend if she can fold it 10 or more times. "Duh, of course!" she'll reply.

2. **Tell her to fold the sheet in half.** Now she has two layers.

3. **Ask her to fold** it again without undoing the first two layers.

What's the Deal?
Folding paper sounds easy, but as the area of the folded paper decreases and the thickness of the folds increases, it becomes really hard. There's a cool math pattern at work here: Fold the paper once and you have two layers, because 1 × 2 = 2. Fold it twice: 2 × 2 = 4. If you could fold it 10 times, you'd be talking 2 to the 10th power, or 1,024 layers of paper. That's too much for even the Hulk to smash flat.

4. **Instruct her to keep folding.** The paper will double and redouble, and she'll call it quits after several more folds.

Little Paper, Great Big You

Can you cut a hole in an ordinary piece of paper that's big enough for you to walk through?

To do this, you gotta enclose a big area (yourself) in a small fixed boundary: a standard sheet of printer paper. Does a square hole work? A circle? No? Here's a clever way to solve the problem.

1 **Fold the paper** in half lengthwise, as in the diagram below. Turn the folded side toward yourself. Put your scissors 1 inch (2.5 cm) from the paper's short edge, and snip into the paper. Stop your cut 1 inch (2.5 cm) from the unfolded side.

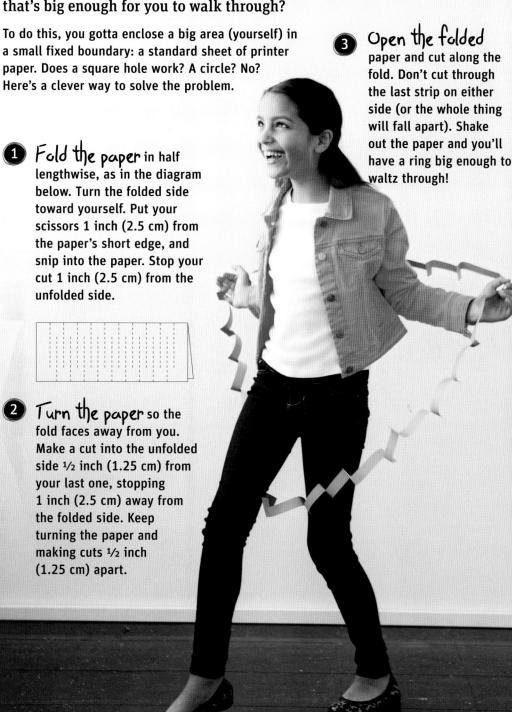

2 **Turn the paper** so the fold faces away from you. Make a cut into the unfolded side ½ inch (1.25 cm) from your last one, stopping 1 inch (2.5 cm) away from the folded side. Keep turning the paper and making cuts ½ inch (1.25 cm) apart.

3 **Open the folded** paper and cut along the fold. Don't cut through the last strip on either side (or the whole thing will fall apart). Shake out the paper and you'll have a ring big enough to waltz through!

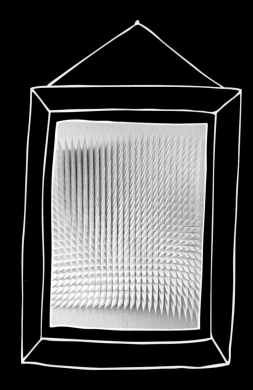

Science Meets Art: Matt Shlian

This paper engineer–artist crosses the ancient art of origami with high-tech computer models to make astonishingly intricate paper sculptures. "There's an immediacy to paper," explains Shlian, who says he's an "explorer and inventor." When he was a kid, he took apart pop-up books to see just how they worked, and later he studied art. "I'm a curious person.," he says. "I did everything…glassblowing, ceramics. I didn't know what I was doing, [but] if nothing is known, everything is possible." Try out Shlian's freewheeling approach to artistic creation: Fold, snip, and stack paper, and explore all the 3-D structures and patterns you can make out of this very simple—but weirdly complex—2-D material.

LAB #07

Recess Research

Whoo-hah! Run outside and shake those arms and legs—and then play around with playground physics, sports secrets, and blacktop brainteasers.

Cyclops basketball! Can you dunk with one eye patched?

The best science experiments are the goofiest. Climb the monkey bars, chuck stuff off the top, and learn all about free-fall.

All your recess running and jumping uses neurons: your nerve cells. You've got 100 BILLION in your brain alone!

"As light as air" is totally bogus. Air's got weight, and you can measure it.

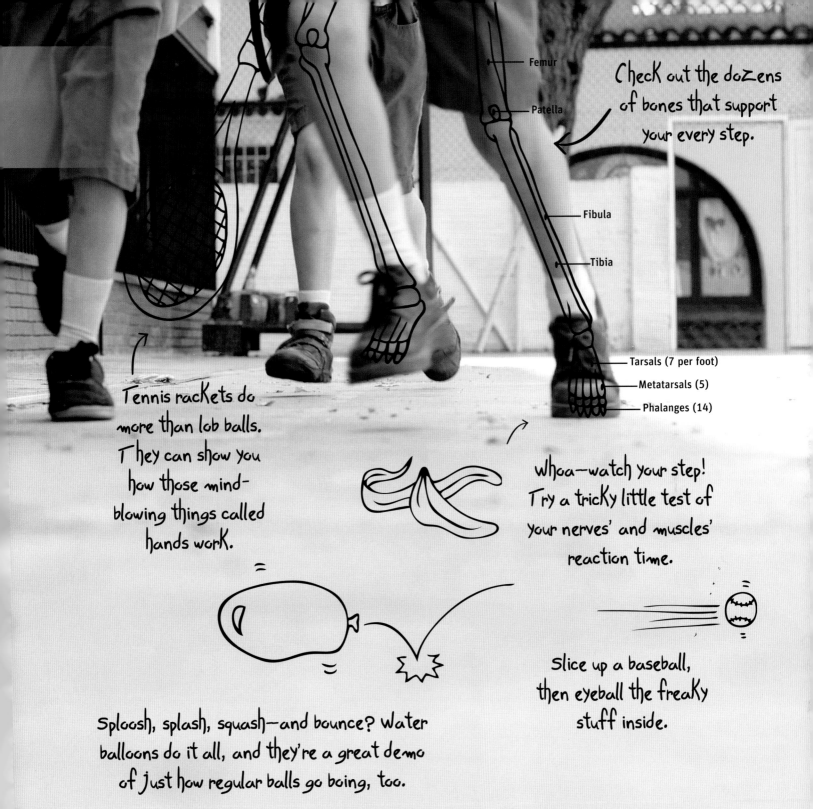

Femur

Patella

Check out the dozens of bones that support your every step.

Fibula

Tibia

Tarsals (7 per foot)

Metatarsals (5)

Phalanges (14)

Tennis rackets do more than lob balls. They can show you how those mind-blowing things called hands work.

Whoa—watch your step! Try a tricky little test of your nerves' and muscles' reaction time.

Sploosh, splash, squash—and bounce? Water balloons do it all, and they're a great demo of just how regular balls go boing, too.

Slice up a baseball, then eyeball the freaky stuff inside.

57

The Pendulum Swing

Pendulums are used in all kinds of machines, from grandfather clocks to playground swings. Hop aboard to see how they operate.

1 *First, sit down* and check out the three basic parts of this recess favorite. Notice its *pivot point*, where the chains attach to the bar. The *pendulum* itself is the chains. And last there's the *bob*, or weight. That's you—even if you're not named Bob!

2 *Pay attention to the motions.* As you propel yourself forward, you lean back and stick out your legs. Your extended body increases air resistance, and your pull on the chains (the pendulum) levers them around the pivot point, so the pendulum's swing grows wider as you work. On the backward swing, you lean forward and tuck your legs. Gravity drags you down easily now because your tucked body creates less air resistance.

3 *Ask a smaller—or bigger—friend* to sit next to you. Does she go faster or slower? Neither! She'll swing at the same pace unless her swing's chains are a different length than yours. The time it takes to complete a swing doesn't depend on how much the bob weighs, but on the length of the pendulum.

Is that tall tale about how some kid swung all the way over the bar true? Nope. Once you swing past 90 degrees, the chains go slack for a second before you drop down. Higher swings mean more slack, so you can't create enough momentum to get over the bar.

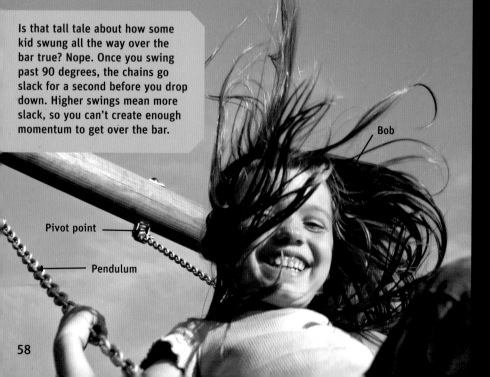

Bob

Pivot point

Pendulum

Bounce a Water Balloon

Can hurling water balloons show you how sports balls bounce? Sure! Because they're squishier and slower-moving than sports balls, water balloons reveal how a real ball changes shape when it hits the ground.

1 *Find a couple of balloons,* then make a burst-proof bouncer by smearing cooking oil on one balloon and shoving it into the second, dry balloon. Fill the inner balloon with water and knot them both.

2 *Drop the balloon ball,* and watch carefully! It builds up energy as gravity pulls it downward. Here's what happens next...

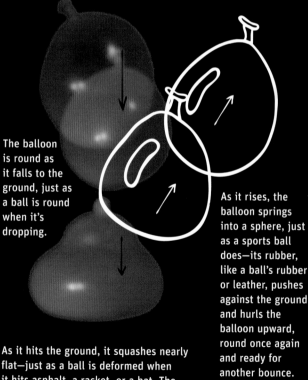

The balloon is round as it falls to the ground, just as a ball is round when it's dropping.

As it rises, the balloon springs into a sphere, just as a sports ball does—its rubber, like a ball's rubber or leather, pushes against the ground and hurls the balloon upward, round once again and ready for another bounce.

As it hits the ground, it squashes nearly flat—just as a ball is deformed when it hits asphalt, a racket, or a bat. The energy generated by its fall is released as the balloon's rubber stretches outward.

Drop It!

Join the proud scientific tradition of watching stuff go *splat* to investigate gravity's peculiar properties.

1. **You need a little pebble,** a big feather, and a place to drop them. The top of the monkey bars works fine, but make sure no one's below!

2. **Hold the feather** in one hand and the pebble in the other. Level out your fists and drop both things at the same time. Which hits the ground first?

What's the Deal?

In a vacuum, the pebble and feather would hit the ground at the same time. But, as you've observed, they don't. The pebble hits first. Why? *Air resistance*. The two objects are falling through the air, and large objects (such as a feather) experience more air resistance than small ones (such as a pebble) do, even if they are lighter than the small ones. So the feather falls slowly. Another reason? *Terminal velocity*. When air resistance just balances gravity's downward pull on an object, the object can't gain any more speed. It's reached its terminal velocity. Since the feather is bigger than the pebble, air resistance on it quickly builds to equal gravity's pull. The feather can't gain more speed, so it just drifts downward. The smaller pebble, meanwhile, must fall farther before it gains enough speed so that air resistance balances gravity's pull on it. The pebble quickly pulls away from the feather and hits the dirt first.

As Heavy as Air

Two balloons of the same size are always the same weight...unless one's filled with air and one isn't.

1. **Use a tape measure** to find the midpoint of a 3-foot- (1-m-) long wood dowel. Mark it in pen.

2. **Blow up** two identical balloons. Tape one to each end of the dowel.

3. **Balance the dowel** at its midpoint on one finger. Ask a friend to slowly stick a pin in one balloon, then *slowly* draw it out—the balloon will gradually deflate, but it won't pop.

4. **Watch your dowel** tilt down toward the intact, inflated balloon. Air, as immaterial as it seems, *does* have weight!

Check Your Balance

What's more fun than spinning in circles or standing on your hands until you collapse in a dizzy heap? Doing it *without* falling over. Hone the connections among your eyes, ears, and brain that keep you balanced with these exercises.

The Ballerina's Secret Weapon

No, she's not armed. But she's got a cool eye trick that keeps her balanced during a quintuple pirouette: *spotting*. She fixes her gaze on a high, stable object and keeps her eyes and head turned toward the object as long as she can while spinning. Then she quickly whips her head around to refocus on the object. This technique keeps fluid in the inner ear (which detects solid and shaky balance, just as our eyes do) from sloshing around and triggering the dizzies.

Try it: Stare at a tree and whip your head as you whirl. How many times can you spin without getting dizzy?

Use Your Eyes

Find a clear patch of grass on the school grounds. Flip into a handstand or headstand, close your eyes, and count the seconds until you flop over.

Now open your eyes, flip upside down again...and stay that way until your arms give out. Your open eyes are now passing details on stable objects—such as the horizon—to your brain, and your brain can use that information to adjust the more than 300 muscles that keep you upright—or upside down. (Not great at being upside down? Try lifting one leg with your eyes closed!)

Put on Your Game Pace

Sports often involve something (a ball) or someone (an opponent) barreling toward you. You need quick reflexes to react, so test your reaction time off-field with this easy game.

1 **Raise your arm**, keeping your thumb and index finger 1 inch (2.5 cm) apart. Ask a friend to place the bottom end of a ruler between them. Then she drops it and you try to grab it.

2 **Look at the ruler** to see where you caught it. The 6-inch (15-cm) mark is the best most of us can do. Why? Look at the kid at right to see just how complex the trip is from your eyes through your nerves to your fingers.

Move your thumb and finger 3 inches (7.5 cm) apart and repeat the test. Can you get the ruler? No? You need about $^1/_5$ second to change visual info into motion—but the ruler needs less time than that to slip through your grasp.

First your eyes register light reflecting off the ruler, and your optic nerves shoot its image to your brain's *occipital* (visual) *lobe*...

The occipital lobe pings the info to your brain's *frontal lobe*, which decides what your muscles will do next....

Your frontal lobe sends an order ("Grab!") to your *motor cortex*, which shoots impulses to your *spinal cord*...

The nerves of the spinal cord carry the motor cortex's command to your arms, hands, and fingers. The nerve impulses travel fast, but they slow down at the junctions between nerves, as well as between nerves and muscles...

Finally your thumb and finger close on the falling ruler!

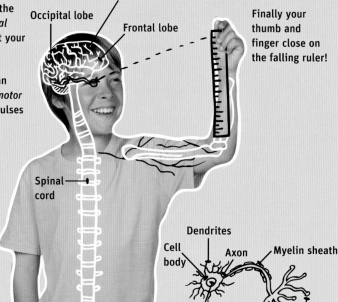

Motor cortex
Occipital lobe
Frontal lobe
Spinal cord

Dendrites
Cell body
Axon
Myelin sheath
Nucleus
Axon terminals

Human neuron

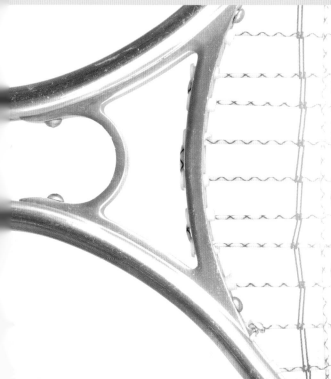

It's All in Your Hands

Hands are one of the features that make us *Homo sapiens*— and their super-sensitive nerves let us do everything from petting a dog to performing brain surgery. Try this experiment to get a sense of how those nerves talk to one another.

1 **Pick up a tennis racket** and rub one hand across its mesh head. No surprises here: You feel the bumpy strings and knots.

2 **Now put your hands together** with the racket in between, one hand on each side of the racket head. Feel an odd velvety sensation? Its cause: confusion among your hands' nerve cells. Your hands feel each other's surface at the same time that they feel the mesh, triggering a weird combination of nerve stimuli that your brain interprets as "soft."

What's in a Baseball? 🔍

Foam? Candy? The ghost of Babe Ruth? Get a craft knife and an official National League ball (the only kind that works for this dissection project), and then scope out the complex layers of this seemingly simple object.

1 **We cut this ball** in half to give you a sneak peek inside, but it's way more fun to unwind the ball starting from its outer leather covering. First cut through the seam's threads, then strip the leather off the ball. A dense layer of thin twine appears.

2 **Peel off** that outer twine layer. Pro balls have dark, heavy yarn underneath; cheap ones sport solid cork or rubber. Unravel the yarn and you'll spot red anchor points for the outer seams.

3 **Here's another layer:** white yarn. If the yarn's wound tightly, the ball is springy. If it's loose, the ball won't fly well when it's hit. Unwind the yarn.

4 **More yarn,** black this time! Spool it away until you uncover a thin red rubber layer.

5 **Slice that rubber layer open,** and you'll see a black rubber layer. Now slice through *that*, and out pops the ball's heart: a tiny cork core, no bigger than a grape.

What's the Deal?

Why do baseballs require so many different layers? Through decades of testing (and sometimes cheating with nonregulation materials), ballmakers and ballplayers developed a near-perfect combination of materials and density, so today's balls are neither too lively nor too dead when walloped by the bat.

Pitch a Polar Baseball

No ball handy? Make one out of paper, plastic, or twine, or use the hub of a worn-out ball!

An old-time pitcher's clever cheat? Freeze a ball for an hour before a big game!

A frozen ball can turn a hit that should've been an outta-sight homer into a pop fly. Why? The air in the ball contracts, as do its materials. The stiffened ball can't flex properly when clobbered by a bat, so it flies about as well a rock.

You won't find today's pitchers doing a freezer fake-out, but in the past, even greats such as Connie Mack sometimes used these icy imposters in tight games.

Play Pirate Ball

Don yer eye patch, matey, and play ball the buccaneer way! Cover one eye with a kerchief or taped-on paper, then find a ball and a basket.

Can you catch passes or score? It's tough! Your *peripheral vision* on the patched eye is gone, so you can't see the ball flying past on that side. Your *depth perception* is out of whack, too: Normally each eye sends your brain a different picture of the same scene to blend into one image. But because one eye is covered up, your brain can't accurately judge distance to other players or to the ball.

Windows and Weather

We all get stuck inside sometimes, especially on rainy days. Take a good long look out the window, and you'll start wondering about the science behind what you see.

If it's stormy, stay in and do raindrop research!

Bottle up a vortex to see how tornadoes and hurricanes work.

Hungry? Snack on a mouthful of lightning bolts!

Conjure up a raging storm... the way movie sound artists do.

Find out how wind shapes the weather—and build a whooshing wind tunnel and fast fliers to soar inside it.

The Sun's a fickle traveler. Sketch its loopy path on the wall.

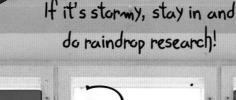

Kraack!

LAB #08

Beat the Bounce

It's a bright old world out there. Sunlight bounces off nonmetallic surfaces and is polarized into glare—but you can vanquish that glare with these special filters.

1 *Put one piece* of the polarized sheet over each eye and turn toward the window (but don't look directly at the Sun).

2 *Rotate each piece.* Does the scenery go dim, then bright? Does the sky turn from pale to deep blue? (Photographers love polarized lenses: They boost color but reduce reflection.)

3 *Look around* to find a flat surface, such as a sidewalk, with lots of glare coming off it. Twist the pieces until they block light bouncing off the sidewalk. You still see the concrete—but its glare is cut. (Anglers love polarized sunglasses: They see fish but not glare off the water.)

4 *Stack the sheets.* Turn them perpendicular to each other so they darken, blocking both horizontally *and* vertically oriented light waves.

Phenomenal Polarized Phun

Make a stupendous stained-glass window—without any glass!

1 *Grab the two sheets* opposite.

2 *Stick bits* of transparent Scotch shipping tape (the only kind that works in this activity) in crisscross patterns on both sheets. Overlap some strips or form words or pictures. Then put the sheets together so their tape faces toward the middle of the "sandwich."

3 *Hold up the sheets* to a window's light. Rotate them in opposite directions. Gorgeous colors and geometric shapes appear and disappear, and the words and pictures slide in and out of view.

What's the Deal?
Polarization is pretty, and also pretty complex. Sunlight (holding all the rainbow's hues) goes through the first polarized sheet, which lets through only light vibrating perpendicular to its molecules. Then the long, stretchy molecules of the tape on the two sheets twist each color of light a different amount. The altered waves then hit the second polarizer—but only colors perpendicular to its molecules can pass through! The end result is a kaleidoscopic play of colors as you rotate each sheet.

Warp Light with Water 🔍

All lenses bend light and magnify or shrink what we see. But lenses needn't be glass or plastic. Ice, water, a raindrop—any clear liquid is a perfect close-focus lens.

On a stormy day, find a ground-floor window without a screen. Open it halfway. Lean out to peer at the side of raindrops clinging to the pane—they're curved outward *(convex)*, just like a lens in a magnifying glass. Use your own magnifier to look at them up close.

Get on your rain boots and get outside. Peek through the same window's droplets: Do they enlarge or reduce objects in the room? Inspect a teeny drop and a big one. Which is the best magnifier?

That's Just the Way It Flows

Raindrops flowing down a window on a rainy day don't trace a straight path. Instead they stop, start, turn, and wiggle. Are they confused or following a pattern? Find out by putting on a drop drag race.

1 Find a buddy and haul him outside. Pick out a rain-streaked window, and then each of you chooses the fattest, fastest-looking drop you can find near the top of the pane. Cheer on your racers!

2 Whose drop reached the windowsill first? Did it squiggle down, or did it roll straight? And did it gobble up any other raindrops along the way?

3 Now you get to cheat by steering your drops. Pick new drop racers, then poke them with your fingers as they run. Can you get them to put on the gas? Do they pick out new routes after you touch them, or just return to their original paths?

What's the Deal?

Champion raindrops are those that "eat" the most other drops on their race to the bottom. If you steer a drop into another one, they *coalesce*: The drops' molecules cling to one another and form a single fatter, heavier drop. You'll also see that once a droplet changes course in one spot, that shift will shape its flow for the rest of its path. In fact, water droplets on glass behave much like rivers on the Earth's surface: Rivers run in *meanders*—curves shaped by obstacles such as mountains and rocky patches in their path—and their speed increases when they meet and eat other, smaller rivers.

Sketch the Sun's Road

The Sun's path across the sky shifts as the seasons turn. Track our star through a whole year—you'll need patience, as every scientist does!—to watch its fascinating figure 8 trail emerge.

1 *Choose a day and time* when you can Sun-chase weekly, and then find a south-facing window. Make sure the Sun will shine through that window at your chosen time.

2 *Set a small mirror* on the windowsill so that beams of sunlight reflect off it onto a blank wall. Tape the mirror to the sill, and ask that no one mess with it—yeah, for a full year!

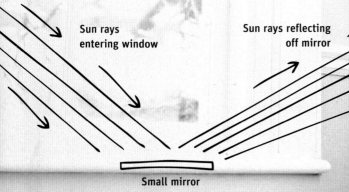

Sun rays entering window

Sun rays reflecting off mirror

Small mirror

3 *On the first day* of your Sun-tracking adventure, put a sticky note on the wall where the reflection hits it. Write the date on the note. Each week at the same time, put another dated sticky on the reflection. (Remember daylight saving time: When you move your clock forward an hour, move your Sun-chasing time forward one hour.)

4 *At year's end,* see which shape your sticky notes make. If your teacher or parents give the okay, lightly trace that pattern in pencil. Do you see a figure 8? That's an *analemma,* showing the Sun's shifting position. It's set by Earth's funky orbit, which is tilted in relation to the Sun.

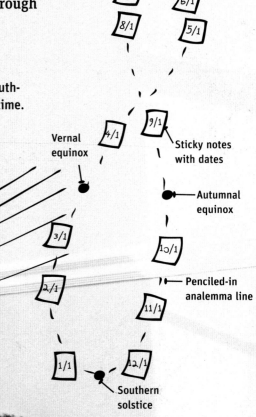

Northern solstice

7/1 6/1
8/1 5/1

9/1

Vernal equinox

4/1

Sticky notes with dates

Autumnal equinox

3/1

10/1

Penciled-in analemma line

2/1

11/1

1/1

12/1

Southern solstice

What's the Deal?

Wonder why the analemma isn't circular? In summer in the Northern Hemisphere, the North Pole tips sunward—the Sun rises north of due east and takes a long, high path through the sky. In winter, the North Pole tips away from the Sun, and the Sun rises south of due east and hikes a short, low course across the sky. Another factor is Earth's *elliptical* (oval) orbit around the Sun. When we lean sunward, Earth orbits faster. When we tilt away, Earth orbits slower. That means the Sun rises at a different spot each day—so the reflection on your wall shifts its position, too.

Bottle a Vortex

Ever spotted a hurricane or tornado? Then you've seen a *vortex*. Capture this cosmic force—without venturing into a storm!—inside a couple of old soda bottles.

Vortexes are found all over nature—they include whirlpools, waterspouts, and even black holes. When air, water, or cosmic matter spins, *centripetal force*, which pulls the substance inward, acts upon it. The faster the substance rotates, the deeper and stronger its central vortex will become.

1 **Fill a 2-L soda bottle** two-thirds full of water. Pour in several drops of food coloring.

2 **Invert another,** empty 2-L plastic bottle on the filled one. Between their mouths, place a washer with a 3/8-inch- (9.5-mm-) wide hole. Tightly seal the bottles' mouths together with duct tape. Some water will drip through the washer, but *surface tension* (water molecules' tendency to stick together) slows the flow.

3 **Now flip the bottles** so the filled one's on top, and rapidly rotate them several times. Watch a vortex form as the water rushes into the empty bottle, gulped down by the amped-up gravity that centripetal force creates in the vortex's center.

Make a Mouthful of Lightning

A few sweet candies let you roar like Thor.

1 *A quick trip* to the candy shop is your first task. Buy several brands of wintergreen-flavored breath mints.

2 *Pull the curtains*, stand in front of a mirror, and switch off the room light.

3 *Stick a candy* on your tongue and—just this once—chew with your mouth wide open. Ghostly blue sparks will bounce around your teeth.

4 *Try another brand.* Which makes the best lightning storm?

What's the Deal?

You're making light with friction! As you chomp, the sugar crystals are stressed and create electric fields strong enough to rip the outer electrons away from their molecules. When the molecules recombine with their electrons, they emit invisible ultraviolet light. But wintergreen oil (methyl salicylate) converts this light into bright blue bolts. For the best Thor imitation, spring for the strongest-flavored candies.

Fake a Thunderclap

Some movie sound effects are added by Foley artists—auditory magicians who use ordinary stuff to make extraordinary noises.

- ☐ Shake sheet metal = Thunder
- ☐ Squeak a leather tool belt = Branches creaking in the wind
- ☐ Shake dried peas in a wooden box = Pouring rain
- ☐ Squeeze a box of cornstarch = Footfalls in deep snow
- ☐ Dump kitty litter slowly onto craft paper = Landslide
- ☐ Flap plastic bags = Rain on gravel
- ☐ Flip over a bike and spin a wheel, holding a silk scarf against it = Whistling wind

Clouds come in any shape you can imagine—and some you probably can't!

Science Meets Art: Berndnaut Smilde

These nimbus clouds live indoors, but only for a second. The artist finds an empty room, controls its temperature and humidity for ideal cloud formation, then puffs a fog machine's vapor into the space. He snaps a photo, and then the nimbus vanishes—an artwork that's as short-lived as real clouds. Smilde's art is spooky and funny because no one expects to see natural phenomena indoors. Can you dream up ways to bring the wild weather inside?

Cirrus

Cirrocumulus

Cumulus

Cumulonimbus

Holepunch

Lenticular

Breeze or Hurricane?

Has the rain cleared up? Head outside to see how fast the wind is blowing with a homemade anemometer.

You'll need:
Hole puncher
5 paper cups
Ruler
Pencil
2 drinking straws
Duct tape
Colored marker
Straight pin
Watch with second hand

① **With the hole puncher,** make four evenly spaced holes in one cup, each ¼ inch (6.5 mm) below its rim. Use the pencil to make another hole in the center of the cup's bottom. Hold the cup up, slide the straws through the holes by the rim, and secure their crossing point with duct tape.

② **Pick another cup.** Punch a hole in it midway between its rim and its bottom. Hold it horizontally and slide one straw's free end into the hole until its inside end touches the cup's opposite wall. Repeat with the other three cups. All the cups' openings must face the same way!

③ **Draw a star** in marker on one horizontal cup. Poke the pencil, eraser side up, into the hole in the center cup's bottom. Then push the straight pin through the straws' crossing point and into the eraser. The pencil and center cup must turn freely, so don't set the pin deeply. Outdoors, firmly stick the anemometer into the dirt, pushing down the pencil point so it stays still.

④ **Sit down** facing the "star" cup. As the wind blows, use your watch to see how many times the star passes you in a minute. If it passes 10 times, the wind's blowing at 10 miles per hour. For kilometers per hour, convert the miles-per-hour reading: 1 mile equals 1.6 km, so multiply the number of miles by 1.6 for the number of kilometers. In this case, 10 miles per hour equals about 16 kilometers per hour.

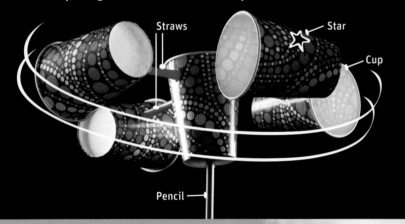

Straws — Star — Cup — Pencil

Which Way Does the Wind Blow?

Forecasters use high-tech gear to check wind direction. But you can do it, too—it's as easy as raising a finger.

① **Look out at midday** to see if leaves or grasses are moving in the breeze. Use a compass to suss out the direction they're blowing in, and write it down. Now go outside, lick a finger, and hold it up. One side will feel cool—the side facing the wind. Does it match your compass reading?

② **Return to the same spot** in early evening. Did the wind switch direction? Probably so if you're near a coast: Cool breezes blow from ocean to land in the daytime (when warm air rises off the land and cool sea air moves in under it) and reverse direction at night (when warm air over the sea makes way for air from the cooling land). Mountains and grassland can cause a similar twilight switcheroo.

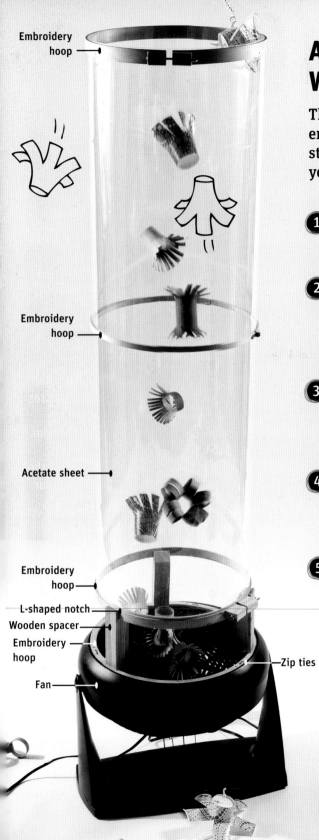

Embroidery hoop

Embroidery hoop

Acetate sheet

Embroidery hoop

L-shaped notch
Wooden spacer
Embroidery hoop

Fan

Zip ties

A Totally Tubular Wind Tunnel

This DIY wind tunnel—like the ones engineers use, but made of household stuff—teaches you about wind even when you're stuck inside.

1 **Lay the fan face up.** Place an embroidery hoop on the fan, attaching it firmly to the fan with zip ties.

2 **Stand the spacers** around the hoop's edges and set a second hoop on top. Pencil a line on each spacer where the upper hoop touches it. Ask an adult to saw an L-shaped notch in each spacer, following the line and making each notch as deep as the hoop edge is tall. Then attach the spacers to the bottom hoop with wood glue.

3 **Roll the acetate** into a cylinder, then slide the three embroidery hoops onto the tube so one is in the middle and one is on both of the far ends. Tighten all the hoops' screws, then join the acetate's inner and outer edges with clear tape.

4 **Stand the acetate** cylinder atop the spacers and wedge its lower embroidery hoop into the L-shaped notches.

5 **Now make whirligigs!** Cut cups into rotor blades, tape tissue paper to craft sticks, or slice cardboard tubes into spirals. Turn the fan to its highest speed and drop your fliers in the tube. Which ones crash? Which ones soar? And which shapes fly best?

You'll need:

Fan, 18 inches (46 cm) across, with an adjustable-tilt head

Four 14-inch (36-cm) wooden embroidery hoops

Three 7-inch (18-cm) zip ties

Three wooden spacers

Saw, and an adult to help you use it!

Wood glue

Thin 4-by-4-foot (122-by-122-cm) acetate sheet

Clear tape

Scissors

Paper cups, cardboard tubes, tissue paper, pipe cleaners, and other whirligig makings

LAB #09

That Big Patch of Grass

...You know the one. It needs mowing, and there aren't any swings or soccer goals—but it's awesome for catch or cartwheels. It's awesome for finding stuff out, too.

Ready for some arith-ma-stick?

Little floaters high up in the sky—how did you get in my eye?

There sure are a lot of bugs about! Track them with a bug journal.

Flowers lead secret lives! Do a dissection to learn about them.

The sky is really blue today. How come?

It's a bird, it's a plane...it's a hoopster!

BZZ! If there are flowers, there are bees. Learn how to make their terrifying sound. (Stinger not included.)

Why does this scarecrow look bigger than that faraway tree?

Organize an awesome ant parade.

Just how many blades of grass are in this field? Count them all!

Do you know what dirt is made of?

Tear Up a Tulip

Time to get your claws into nature: Shred yourself a flower to learn about what's hiding inside those pretty petals.

2 **Tear off each leaf and petal** and spread them on the paper. Play detective with the petals, eyeing them with the magnifying glass. Can you spot any dotted nectar guides? These are signs saying, "Hey, over here!" to lure in pollinator bugs.

1 **Before you start ripping,** suss out the whole flower with a magnifying glass. Shake it over black paper and zero in on a pollen grain.

Stigma

Stamen

Get the Dirt on Dirt

Not all soil is the same. Some is sandy, some's silty, some's mostly clay. Don't know what's under your feet? Test it to find out.

Okay, we give you permission to get *really* dirty. Scoop up a great big handful of dirt from an empty lot or community garden and squeeze it as hard as you can. If it crumbles right away, it's sandy soil. If it sticks together in a wad, complete with finger imprints, it's clay soil. If it falls apart slowly, it's probably a mixture of sand, clay, and silt: the three main soil types.

Which type is best for plants? A mix! They grow best in dirt that has some sand to help drain extra water, silt for yummy minerals, and clay to hold water and the organic stuff that makes plants fat and happy. Look around—are there healthy plants in your field?

3. **Pull off a stamen,** then pluck a stigma. Squish them. Does the stamen leave pollen on your fingers? Is the stigma sticky? Visiting bugs pick up pollen from stamens and then deposit it on sticky stigmas. Later: baby tulips!

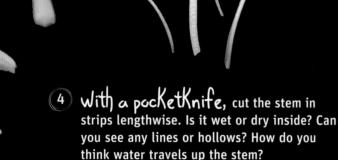

Stamen

4. **With a pocketknife,** cut the stem in strips lengthwise. Is it wet or dry inside? Can you see any lines or hollows? How do you think water travels up the stem?

Science Meets Art: Kathy Klein

Klein sets flower petals in patterns called *mandalas* and leaves them behind for lucky people to find. You can create your own artwork by arranging petals in a circle, star, or abstract design. Like it? Try patterns made with rocks, leaves, sticks, sand, and all the other stuff on nature's craft table.

1. **To figure out** your soil's exact type, mix up mud potion at home! Fill a clear quart (0.95-L) jar two-thirds full of water, toss in a teaspoon of water softener (such as Calgon), and fill the rest with interesting dirt. Cap the jar and shake until your arms get tired. Set the jar where your little brother can't mess with it, wait a week, and then peek. You'll see several layers.

2. **Draw lines on the jar** in permanent marker to separate the layers, then measure each one to see which is thickest. That layer tells you the soil's main type.

The top layer will likely be clay. It falls out of the mud potion last. (Coarse crud floating above the clay layer is just rotted grass and leaves.)

Floury silt particles drift down before clay. They're small, about 0.002 to 0.05 mm across.

This stuff down here? Sand. It falls out of the mud potion first because it has big, gritty particles (0.05 to 2.0 mm across).

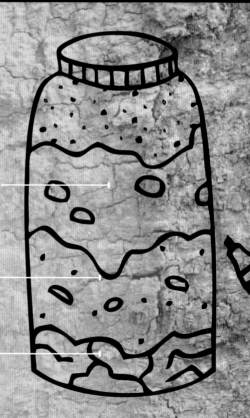

Loop-the-Loop with a Hoopster

Most paper planes look like flattened versions of the skyracers that you see crisscrossing the heavens every day, but the one you're about to make is all circles and, man, can it go!

You'll need:
Scissors
3-by-5-inch (7.5-by-12.5-cm) index cards
Ruler
Clear plastic tape
Plastic straws (not the bendy kind)

1 Cut an index card the long way into three equal strips, each 1 inch (2.5 cm) wide and 5 inches (12.5 cm) long.

2 Curl one strip into a little hoop and tape its ends together.

3 Tape the other two strips together end to end to make one long strip. Curl this strip into a hoop and tape its ends together, too.

4 Thread the big hoop onto one end of the straw. Smooth a piece of tape over the straw end and up the insides of the hoop to secure it in place.

5 Thread the small hoop onto the other end of the straw. Attach it to the straw with a piece of tape.

6 Now comes the fun! Hold the hoopster in the middle of the straw, with the little hoop facing front. Throw it like a paper airplane. It may take a little practice, but once you get the hang of it, your hoopster will really fly!

Plastic straw

Little paper hoop

Big paper hoop

Variation with two straws

Add a paper clip to one hoop to see how the hoopster flies with cargo. Or use two straws for a really long hoopster, or a double model with two hoops side by side on each end.

Variation with paper clip

Spot Curious Specks in the Sky

Guess what: You've got tiny, tiny garbage floating around in your eyes.

Hey, you! Stop running around for just a second. Lie down, relax, and look up at the sky or the clouds (not the Sun!). After a while, you'll see tiny shapes in the air—light, clear circles or threads.

These are *floaters,* and they're bits of junk drifting in the liquid near your retina, the layer of light-sensitive cells at the back of your eyeball. When you lie down, the floaters sink toward your retina and may settle into the *fovea,* the area where your vision is sharpest.

How did these pieces of junk get into your eye? They're leftover bits of structures and cells that were part of your eye before you were born. Close one eye, then the other—can you still see them?

Make a Sky-in-a-Box

The sky actually isn't blue—the atmosphere just tricks your eyes into thinking it is. Build this sky-in-a-box to see how the trick works!

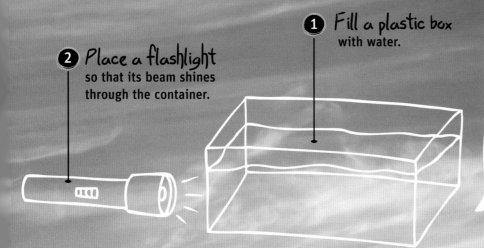

1 Fill a plastic box with water.

2 Place a flashlight so that its beam shines through the container.

3 Add powdered milk a pinch at a time and stir until you can see the beam shining through the liquid.

4 Look at the beam from the side of the tank—the beam looks bluish-white, just like the sky!

What's the Deal?

The Sun's light may look white, but it's really made up of all the rainbow's colors: red, orange, yellow, green, blue, indigo, and violet. Each one is a wave of energy with its own wavelength—some waves (like red light on one end of the spectrum) travel in long, leisurely swells, while others (like violet light on the spectrum's opposite end) make their way in short, choppy crests. Regardless of its wavelength, each type of light collides with tiny gas molecules on its way through Earth's atmosphere, and these gas molecules "scatter" it—spreading it around. But since the atmosphere's molecules are so small, they're especially good at scattering types of light with short wavelengths. And since blue light has a supershort wavelength, it gets scattered all around the heavens— and that's why the sky looks the way it does.

The Size-and-Distance Illusion

People and creatures off in the distance might look tiny as bugs, even though your smart brain knows they're not. Explore how your mind makes sense of faraway things with this cattle conundrum.

1 Check out this photo of three cows. Which one do you think is biggest? Which one is smallest?

2 Probably you guessed that two of the cows—the one at left and the one at far right—are about the same height. Your brain "sees" the cow at the far right the way it sees all stuff in the background: as a distant object. And, unconsciously, your brain increases its *idea* of that cow's size to make up for its distance away from you.

3 Maybe you also figured that the third cow, the one closest to you, is also the shortest. Sorry, brain. Haul out a ruler and compare it to the cow on the far right. They're actually the same size!

What's the Deal?

When your eyes see an object in the foreground, your brain assumes it is near you—in this case, that the small foreground cow is its real size. So you're fooled into thinking that it and the background cow are different sizes. Luckily, this brain-boggle isn't often a problem in the world outside this book. But people who've lived mostly in crowded places can suffer from a similar optical illusion: They see faraway objects as tiny because they haven't dealt with big distances. In the 1950s, when scientist Colin Turnbull showed a forest-dwelling African Pygmy man his first grassland, the man thought that distant buffalo were little bugs!

Why the Ants Go Marching

Flop on the grass to explore the realm of creepy-crawlies. You'll see flies, spiders, beetles—and ants, marching while other bugs bumble about. Run a simple test to see why they're so organized.

1 Find a smooth patch of dirt with ants on it. Drop some honey in its center, and wait. Soon an ant will stop for a snack, then walk off. Eventually an ant highway will run from the honey to the ants' nest. Each ant marks its path with scent chemicals (*pheromones*) that say, "Free honey this way!" to other ants.

2 Fiddle with their scent road to see how they react. First sprinkle dirt over it. Are the ants confused? How long do they take to find the honey again? Put down a stone to see if these determined creatures find a way around it. Can you wipe away the path with your hand, or do the ants just keep marching?

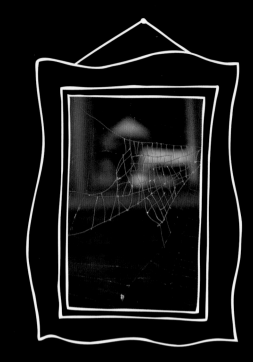

Begin a Bug Book 🔍

Bugs do it all in the grass—getting born, finding food, making babies, dying off—and it's easy to spy on their secret world.

Round up a notebook to use as your bug journal, then gather a glass jar, the magnifier from this book, and a camera and pencil. Dig in moist dirt, overturn stones, and poke along the grassy strips between sidewalks and roads, places where insects can thrive. Scoop a bug into your jar, draw it or snap a pic, and record its location and what it was up to. Then open the jar and say farewell.

Put your bug mugshot here	Where'd you find it?	What was it doing?	What kind of insect do you think it is?
	On dead log, County Road 5	Cleaning its feet!	Dragonfly

Buzz Like a Bee

ZrrrzzzZZZ! You know what that means: Run! Cranky bees are on the move. Imitate their fearsome sound with this simple spinning gizmo.

You'll need:
Craft stick
2 cap erasers
Index card
Scissors
Heavy-duty stapler
2 feet (60 cm) string
Wide, long rubber band

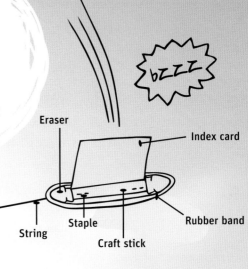

bZZZ

Eraser

Index card

String

Staple

Craft stick

Rubber band

1 **Cover each end** of the craft stick with a cap eraser.

2 **Trim the index card** so its long edge sits neatly between the erasers. Staple its edge to the stick. It should stick out about 2 inches (5 cm).

bZZZZ

5 **Find a clear space** and then swing your humz-o-matic around and around your head.

6 **Can you hear the bees?** Experiment: Spin faster and slower, and bend, slit, or fold the index card. How does the sound change now?

3 **Securely tie the string** onto the craft stick next to one eraser.

4 **Stretch the rubber band** around the stick, from one eraser to the next.

What's the Deal?

When you swing your bee buzzer, moving air vibrates the rubber band, producing sound that the index card amplifies. Real bees buzz in a similar way: They beat their wings as they fly, creating vibrations in the air that we hear as buzzing. Big bees fly slowly, so their buzz is low. Little ones zip around and *bizz* more than *buzz*.

Quick! Arith-Ma-Stick!

Lazing around in a field is great—but you can exercise your brain cells here, too. Pick up a handful of sticks, find a friend, and solve this brain-teaser. (Cover the answer at the bottom of the page, then flip the book upside down to see if you got it correct!)

1 **Arrange 16 twigs** in 5 squares, in the pattern shown below. Your friend then does the same with his own set of 16 sticks.

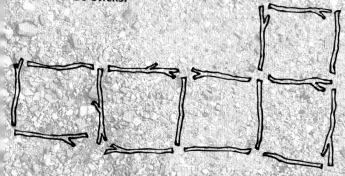

2 **Now it's race time.** Your challenge: See who can first shift just three sticks to make four squares. (It's easier than you think.)

3 **Confused?** Here's a hint: None of the four squares can share a side.

Answer:

A Bazillion Blades of Grass

A sure way to awe your friends: Tell 'em you can count all the grass blades in a field. It's totally doable, so hunker down and get started!

1 **Use the map** to figure out the field's size. With a rectangular field, multiply the length of the shorter side by the length of the longer one. For example, a field that's 100 by 75 feet (30.5 by 23 m) contains about 7,500 square feet (701.5 sq m). If your field's an irregular shape, guesstimate its size.

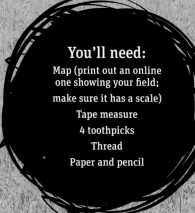

You'll need:

Map (print out an online one showing your field; make sure it has a scale)

Tape measure

4 toothpicks

Thread

Paper and pencil

2 **Okay, how many square inches** are in a square foot (or square centimeters in a square meter)? That's easy: 12 x 12 inches = 144 square inches (and 100 x 100 cm = 10,000 sq cm).

3 **How many square inches** or centimeters are in your field? For feet, multiply 144 by the field's square feet: 7,500 square feet contain 1,080,000 square inches. For centimeters, multiply by 10,000: 701.5 sq m contain 7,015,000 sq cm.

4 **Use your tape measure** to stake off 1 square inch or centimeter of the field. Stick the toothpicks at the square's corners and then loop the thread around them to mark the square.

5 **Start ripping!** Pull up every grass blade in the teeny square and write down the count. Multiply it by the square inches or centimeters in your field, and dazzle your friends with one *very* large number.

LAB #10

All Around Your Downtown

Vroom! Hiding here in the urban bustle are chances to learn about velocity, vision, structural principles, and human behavior—all at a heart-pumping pace.

Weeooo! Weeeooooo!

Is that fire truck screaming closer or wailing away? The Doppler effect knows.

This spinning disc is a phenakistoscope—look right to put it into action!

It's a hard-knock life for a downtown bird. Learn how architects help them avoid collisions.

The wheels on the bike go round and round—but just how does this little zoomster work?

Why are there no 1,000-story skyscrapers? Build your own to find out.

No heaving on the highway! A road-sickness trick can help.

A zooming taxi can act like a tiger—at least in your peripheral vision.

The Urban Whirl

The motion and energy of downtown can play tricks on your eyes. So, too, can this snazzy but simple gizmo: a phenakistoscope. Don't fuss with pronouncing it. Just pluck it off the opposite page and start playing!

A phenakistoscope is an old-timey cinematic device that uses a spinner, evenly placed slots, and a series of slightly altered pictures to fool your eyes into seeing its separate images as a single animated sequence.

1 To use your 'scope, stick a thumbtack through the dot in the disk's center and into the side of a pencil's eraser (look at the picture below). Stand before a mirror and hold up the pencil so you can see the disk's pictures in the mirror. Close one eye and use the other to peer through a slot in the disk.

2 Quickly whirl the disk around with your free hand to watch the leaves tumble in the wheel's imaginary wind—move closer to or farther from the mirror until you can really see the effect roll. Your eyes and brain retain each image on the disk for $1/30$ second, combining them into an illusion of smooth motion. That's called *persistence of vision*—the same thing that brings a movie screen's flickering images to life before our gullible eyes.

3 Now turn the disk to its blank back and use a dry-erase marker to draw an image on each of its 10 petals. The pictures—a speeding train, a hand playing yo-yo (as in the example here), or whatever you like—should progress in a natural sequence. Pin the disk to the pencil eraser, with your "movie" facing the mirror. Spin and watch!

Marvelous Mysterious Motionmobiles

Stuck in traffic? Awesome! Cars, buses, and trains are the greatest toys in the world—you can sing, play guessing games, and fool with fundamental physical forces as you ride along.

On roller coasters, you shut your eyes and scream gleefully as you whip along the track, pulled and pushed by the basic laws of physics. You can try the same thing in a car or bus (minus the screaming, of course).

❶ When the vehicle starts, close your eyes so you can pay more attention to your movements. Notice how you're pressed back into your seat? That's *inertia:* the tendency of an object to keep doing whatever's it doing (in this case, sitting still). It's one of Isaac Newton's basic laws of motion—you start moving only when something makes you move.

❷ When the car or bus stops, you'll notice that you continue hurtling forward until something—your seat belt or friction between your butt and the seat—stops you. Up pops Newton again to remind you that stuff in motion stays in motion until it's stopped.

❸ What happens when the vehicle turns a corner? Your body will keep going forward until friction or the belt drags you sideways, too, pulling you along to follow the path of the car. Now if only your parents would drive you to the amusement park, not physics class!

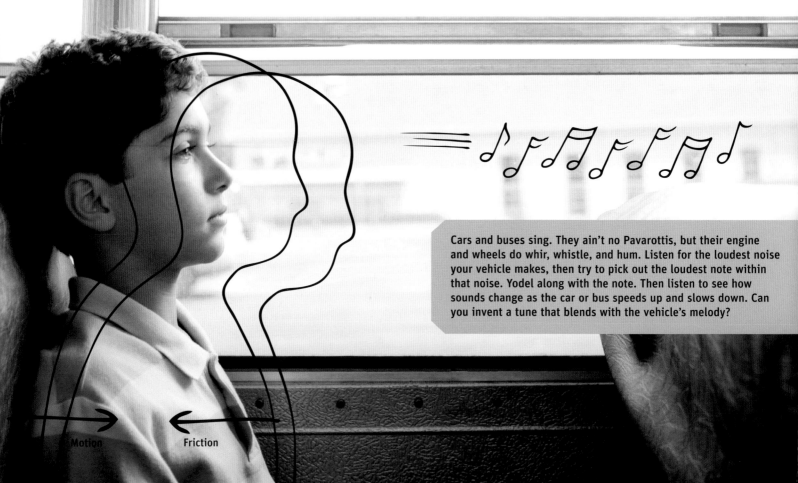

Motion ⟶   ⟵ Friction

Cars and buses sing. They ain't no Pavarottis, but their engine and wheels do whir, whistle, and hum. Listen for the loudest noise your vehicle makes, then try to pick out the loudest note within that noise. Yodel along with the note. Then listen to see how sounds change as the car or bus speeds up and slows down. Can you invent a tune that blends with the vehicle's melody?

The Road Barf Remedy

When you get carsick, blame your ears and eyes, not your tummy.

On a drive, your eyes focus on objects inside the car, which don't appear to be moving. But your inner ear *knows* that you're moving because it senses acceleration. The eye info and ear info argue in your brainstem, where something weird happens: Your brain assumes that either your eyes or ears are hallucinating, decides that poison must be the cause, and tells your stomach to barf it up. To settle the argument—and your tummy—gaze at a steady object on the horizon, such as an electrical tower.

Gear Up

You ride your bike so much it's almost part of you. But how does this stupendously smart machine work? Get to know two of its key parts: the gears and the chain, which help you push power to the max.

1 **Roll out** your bike and shift its gears so the chain is on the smallest cog in front and the largest cog in back. Mark the rear tire's top with a piece of chalk.

2 **Ask a friend** to hold the bike up as you hand-crank the pedals one full turn. How many times does the rear wheel spin? Now shift gears so the largest one is in front, the smallest in back. How many spins per pedal turn do you get?

3 **Put on your helmet** and ponder which gear combination's best for climbing a hill and which one's good for a flat-street sprint. Hit the saddle to road-test your answers!

What's the Deal?

Without its chain drive and gears, the bike we know today would be…well, the one that we knew in the nineteenth century, when riders sat over a big front wheel and one turn of the pedals made that wheel turn once. This made hill climbs hard and even flat riding slow. But gears tweaked the old formula to give you the most roll for your money. Two toothed cogs, one little, one big, interlock with the chain drive, which transfers the foot power you apply to the pedals to the back wheel. Choose a gear that lets you turn the pedals many times to rotate the back wheel just once on uphills, or one that lets you pedal just once for many rotations on downhills. See? More speed, less work!

Science Meets Art: Liz Hickok

This gleaming city scene isn't made of jewels or glass. Hickok casts her incredibly detailed skylines out of...Jell-O. Yup. The brightly colored dessert gelatin is perfect for sculpture not only because it's beautiful when illuminated, but because it reveals cities, which seem big and permanent, as the changeable, sometimes wobbly, always wonder-inspiring places that they really are. The scale model here, of the Palace of Fine Arts in San Francisco (former home of the Exploratorium), suggests both the earthquakes that plague the city and the colorful high spirits of its people. Take a look around your town: Which material would you choose to represent it?

Build a Tiny Skyline

Check out all the towering buildings in your city. How can they reach so high while supporting so much weight? Back at home, find out by crafting the tallest freestanding tower you can. (Then play Godzilla and mash it down.)

1 Cover a table with newspaper and dump ½ pound (227 g) of modeling clay in the middle.

2 Use any method you like—stacked blocks, rolled-out pillars, flattened floors—to put together a skyscraper.

3 When the structure twists and topples, note the problem's source. Did the tower collapse from the top? Or did the middle slump inward first?

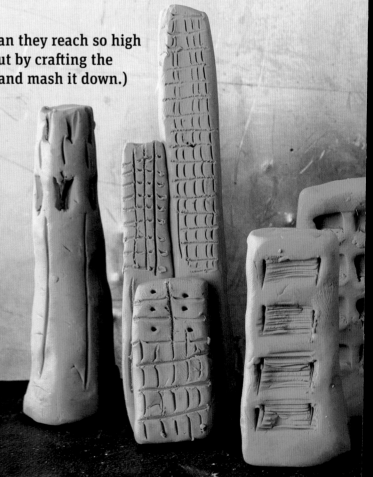

Transparent *and* Reflective

When you window-shop, you can see things and people through store windows, and you can also admire your own reflection in those windows. No duh, but why can you do *both*?

Glass is transparent because it doesn't absorb most light visible to humans. Its molecules' electrons can't absorb much energy when *photons* (or packets of light energy) whack into them. Most photons zip through glass molecules, bounce off stuff in the store, and return to your eyes. But glass—it's crazy stuff!—is also reflective, because molecules on its surface do bounce back a smidgen of visible light. (That's why people always fuss with their hair in front of windows.)

Glass's dual nature is great for us, but lousy for birds. See all those sad lumps at the base of skyscrapers? They're birds that flew into windows. Birds can see glass only one way: reflective at night, or transparent during the day. But clever engineers are helping out. They etch patterns on building glass, cover it with decorative film, or install glass that reflects ultraviolet light (which birds see, but humans can't), all of which lets birdies flap safely away.

4 *Add another* ½ *pound* (227 g) of clay to the table. Can you make a taller tower now? If your new tower tumbles, try a different shape, such as a slender spire, a stepped or tapered pyramid, or a supporting archway. Why do you think some shapes work while others do not?

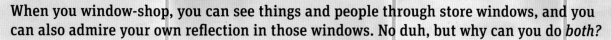

What's the Deal?

Fat bottoms and tiny heads: That's what the world's tallest skyscrapers have. In other words, they're wide at the base and taper at the top. If your building doesn't follow this principle, it's likely to fall. Floors near street level must be broad and beefy to bear the burden of the floors above them; those up top can be narrow and small. And the whole thing must be symmetrical for even weight distribution. So you probably figured out that using twice as much clay didn't let you build a tower twice as tall. To support the added weight, you'd have to use *lots* of extra clay and build a very wide base. You can't scale structures up proportionally and have them work as small structures do—which is just one of the many problems architects solve every day.

Screamin' Sirens

Next time a fire engine wails by downtown, don't shield your ears. Stop to size up its shriek.

1 **As the truck nears you,** cup a hand to one ear. Sound—the energy produced when air molecules smash together—is measured in wavelengths. The engine's motion toward you smooshes the siren's wavelengths together, so it sounds louder and higher in pitch as it draws nearer. That's called the *Doppler effect*.

2 **As the engine passes,** drop your hand. For a second the siren sounds exactly "right": It has the volume and pitch that its manufacturer built into it.

3 **As the engine rushes away,** switch ears. The siren recedes, its sound wavelengths spread out, and the pitch gets lower. But the siren makes exactly the same sound it always did. The only thing that changed? It's now going away from you!

Crosswalk Your Eyes

Vehicles blazing past you are easier to see out of the corner of your eye than ones that are stopped for a red light—a great example of how peripheral vision helps us survive the urban jungle.

1 **Hold a colorful object**—such as a yellow tennis ball—in one outstretched hand. Look straight ahead. Slowly move the ball to one side, but continue to stare straight ahead. Stop when you can't see the ball off to the side of your vision.

2 **Still staring ahead,** with the ball off to the side, move the ball up and down a bit. Suddenly you'll see it again, though you didn't shift your head or eyes.

3 **Does the ball** still look yellow as it moves? Can you see any of its details, such as the seams?

What's the Deal?

Evolution shaped our eyes to be hypersensitive to motion so we could dodge saber-toothed cats leaping from trees and spot tasty deer running past. Our eyes pick up motion nearly everywhere in our visual field, including *peripheral* (edge) areas. But we see color only in a narrow angle, and details in a narrower angle still. That's okay: It doesn't matter whether a predator—or a city bus—is green or red, stripy or plain. All that really matters is that we get out of its way!

Look! Up in the Sky!

We might seem to be thousands of individuals scurrying around, but we're also hypersocial creatures, as watchful of one another as animals on the veldt. Here's a fun way to prove our communal nature to yourself.

1 **Find a busy street.** Stop stock-still on a crowded part of the sidewalk.

2 **Sl-o-o-wly crane your head** upward and stare at the top of a building. Work your look: Let your mouth hang open, bug out your eyes, and gasp.

3 **Watch passersby** out of the corner of your eye. First one will glance up. Then another. Soon one or two will stop to stare with you. Not everyone will pause, but you'll soon collect a decent crowd of fellow gawpers, all of them eager to know just what you've spotted.

Scramble the Sidewalk

Combine two pavement squares into one with this color-contrast trick.

1 **Pick two adjoining squares** of the same color, one a bit lighter than the other. Put your hand before your eyes, edge-on and upright, to hide the border between them.

2 **Look at their colors**—can you tell them apart? When the boundary between two close shades of the same color is hidden, your eyes and brain might tell you they're identical. Lower your hand and look at the squares again. They'll "jump" back to their actual hues. Your vision is very sensitive to areas where brightness falls off or changes, and the visible border triggers this sensitivity.

Multitudes of Maps

In the city, maps help you find streets, subway lines, and the fastest routes and smartest shortcuts. But maps can do so much more, too—they chart emotions and memories, organize data into picture form, describe worlds that don't even exist, and hint at the wondrous places inside our minds.

Sand map

From Middle Earth to Hogwarts to fantasylands of your own creation, maps of fictional places help you imagine yourself in magical locations. What strange, mysterious worlds could you invent on paper?

Any kind of material can be made into a map. Sculpt 3-D maps from sand and earth, such as the "mountain range" above, or arrange ordinary stuff—like toy building blocks—into the shapes of whole continents.

Map of imaginary land

HOGWARTS
School of Witchcraft and Wizardry

1 Boathouse
2 Entrance Courtyard
3 Great Hall
4 Marble Staircase
5 The Quad
6 Viaduct
7 Stone Bridge
8 Headmasters Office
9 Hospital Wing
10 Clock Courtyard
11 Covered Bridge
12 Stone Circle
13 Gamekeeper Hut
14 Owlery
15 Astronomy Wing
16 Dark Tower
17 Library
18 Middle Tower
19 The long Gallery
20 Bell Towers
21 Hufflepuff Basement
22 Gryffindor Tower
23 Ravenclaw Tower
24 Bridge
25 Middle Courtyard
26 Quidditch Pitch
27 Loch
28 Forbidden Forest

South America in Legos

Map of
your day

Maps don't always show places. They can depict time, as the artist above did, showing how she moves through her day from morning toothbrushing to bedtime books. And they can display the way that history reshapes cities, too—the mapmaker below makes 3-D sculptures of city streets to show how roads are built one atop another over the years.

Changing
Portland

Languages
of London

Maps can be "pictures" of all kinds of information—from real data, such as city neighborhoods colored according to the languages their residents speak, to fanciful information, such as the places in town where you think your gloves might have vanished!

Map of
lost stuff

Wonder about the Water

There's as much to learn in the watery world of seas, lakes, and creeks as there is sand on their shorelines. So come on in—the water's fine!

How does a boat float? A few leaves and twigs can teach you the basics of buoyancy.

What does a rubber ducky know about the way the ocean works? Lots!

Turn your favorite skipping rock into a musical stone-a-phone.

Investigate the trash washing up on your shores—and figure out where it comes from.

Just how far underwater can a person dive?

Earth's water came here from deep space—maybe.

Why is water wet, anyway? Because it's sticky!

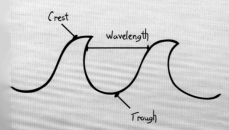

Crest
Wavelength
Trough

Learn wave geometry, which any surfer worth her board wax knows!

Where Did Water Come From?

Not from clouds, scientists theorize, but from deepest, darkest outer space.

Baby stars are one likely source. They hatched out of megaclouds of gas and dust, which also carried water. Ice formed on the dust particles, the dust clumped into planets, and lucky new Planet Earth incorporated a lot of that icy rock and belched out liquid water in its early volcanoes.

Another likely source is comets—speeding iceballs—that bombarded Earth and fed its forming oceans. Asteroids, too, clobbered the young planet, spilling water across the land and helping to fill newborn oceans.

How Waves Behave

Head waterward on a windy day to investigate the world of waves.

1 **Pick out something** bobbing in the swells: a seagull, driftwood, a surfer. Nada? Hurl out a branch.

2 **When the object bobs** all the way up, it's at the wave's *crest*. When it slides down between waves, it's in the *trough*. The distance between two crests? That's the *wavelength*. All waves have this structure.

3 **Notice something weird?** Unless a breaking wave catches your object, it won't move shoreward. It just slides up and down, crest to trough. That's because waves are just flows of energy—they don't move the water itself forward, but make it move like a wheel spinning in place.

Satellites and computers are pro water-watchers' tools, but oceanographers also learn about the sea from stuff that falls off cargo ships. In 1992, 29,000 rubber duckies washed into the Pacific, and the Big Sneaker Spill of 1990 dumped 80,000 shoes in the sea. Scientists found them washed up in amazingly distant places and used that data to map ocean currents.

Why Water's Wet

Kick off your shoes, splash in the shallows, and ask yourself this: Why is water wet, not grainy or globby or dry? Because it's sticky!

Its molecules—which are made of two hydrogen atoms and one oxygen atom—have a negative electrical charge at one end and a positive charge at the other end. And because opposite charges attract each other, the molecules gather into droplets, a process that's called *cohesion*.

When you splash in the water, your skin's molecules break the water molecules' cohesion and draw them toward you. That "stickiness" is called *adhesion*, and it makes water feel wet.

H_2O molecule

Oxygen atom (−)

Hydrogen atoms (+)

How Low Can You Go?

Tubeworms, sea stars, and other deep-sea denizens hang out deep underwater. But air-breathing animals dive to awesome depths, too.

Animal	How far down can it go?	How long can it hold its breath?
Human (free-diving record holder William Trubridge)	397 feet (121 m)	4 minutes, 9 seconds
Cormorant (bird)	200 feet (61 m)	5 minutes
Sperm whale (mammal)	3,280 feet (1,000 m)	85 minutes
Leatherback turtle (reptile)	4,200 feet (1,280 m)	90s minutes
Elephant seal (mammal)	4,921 feet (1,500 m)	2 hours

Grow Some Glow

You'll need:
Wide, clear, lidded plastic container

Starter culture of bioluminescent dinoflagellates (order it from an aquatic-supply website)

Algae growth solution (ditto)

Desk lamp with a 40-watt incandescent bulb

On the beach at dusk, you might spot strange lights in the sand or in the water. Stir up this spooky glow at home to find out how it works.

1 Choose a room that won't get very hot or cold. Carefully wash and dry the container and set it on a flat surface.

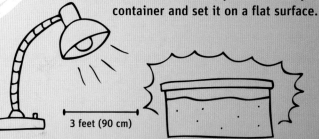

3 feet (90 cm)

2 Let the growth solution and starter culture come to room temperature. Pour in 1 inch (2.5 cm) of growth solution, then add all the starter culture. Put on the lid and shake the container slightly.

3 Set the lamp 3 feet (90 cm) away from the container, as shown in the drawing at left. Don't put the lamp directly over the container, or the solution will overheat. Set up a schedule: Your "dinos" need 12 hours of light and 12 hours of darkness in each 24-hour period, so make sure you don't miss lights-on or lights-out times.

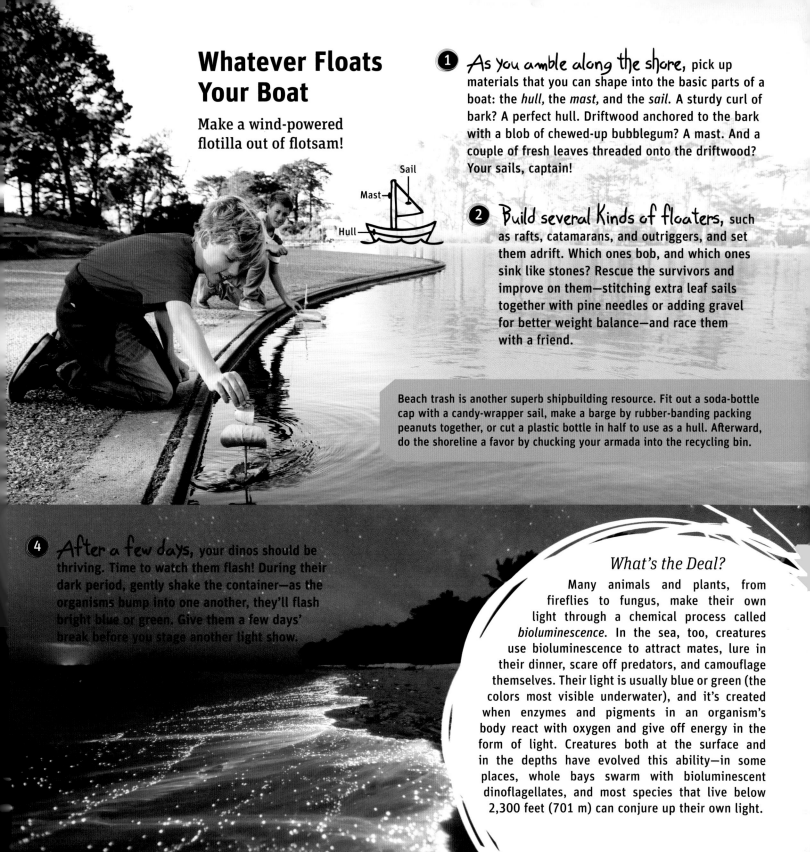

Whatever Floats Your Boat

Make a wind-powered flotilla out of flotsam!

1 *As you amble along the shore,* pick up materials that you can shape into the basic parts of a boat: the *hull*, the *mast*, and the *sail*. A sturdy curl of bark? A perfect hull. Driftwood anchored to the bark with a blob of chewed-up bubblegum? A mast. And a couple of fresh leaves threaded onto the driftwood? Your sails, captain!

Sail
Mast
Hull

2 *Build several kinds of floaters,* such as rafts, catamarans, and outriggers, and set them adrift. Which ones bob, and which ones sink like stones? Rescue the survivors and improve on them—stitching extra leaf sails together with pine needles or adding gravel for better weight balance—and race them with a friend.

Beach trash is another superb shipbuilding resource. Fit out a soda-bottle cap with a candy-wrapper sail, make a barge by rubber-banding packing peanuts together, or cut a plastic bottle in half to use as a hull. Afterward, do the shoreline a favor by chucking your armada into the recycling bin.

4 *After a few days,* your dinos should be thriving. Time to watch them flash! During their dark period, gently shake the container—as the organisms bump into one another, they'll flash bright blue or green. Give them a few days' break before you stage another light show.

What's the Deal?

Many animals and plants, from fireflies to fungus, make their own light through a chemical process called *bioluminescence.* In the sea, too, creatures use bioluminescence to attract mates, lure in their dinner, scare off predators, and camouflage themselves. Their light is usually blue or green (the colors most visible underwater), and it's created when enzymes and pigments in an organism's body react with oxygen and give off energy in the form of light. Creatures both at the surface and in the depths have evolved this ability—in some places, whole bays swarm with bioluminescent dinoflagellates, and most species that live below 2,300 feet (701 m) can conjure up their own light.

"Star" sand of tiny shells

Use this book's magnifier to examine sand grains' unique structure.

Pink coral sand

Beach-glass sand

Magnetic sand

Ooid sand with spherical grains

Is the Coast Clear?

Humans chuck everything in the sea: plastic, old cars, you name it! Tons of trash wash up daily worldwide, menacing ocean and beach life alike. Collect junk on your shore and try to guess its source.

① **Wear heavy gloves** as you gather the junk. Once you've got a bagful, dump it away from the waterline. Divide it into natural debris (sticks, weeds, dead crabs) and human-made stuff.

② **Sort the human junk** into categories, such as cans, plastic bags, cigarette butts, and fishing castoffs like lines and net pieces.

③ **In a journal,** write down the category and the number of each sort of trash that you find, plus the places where you found it. What kinds of items make up most of the garbage? Can you guess how all of this trash found its way onto your beach?

④ **Compare your counts** to the ones here, from a 2011 worldwide beach cleanup. Are your top-five categories the same?

What kind of trash is it?	Where'd you find it?	Count	How do you think it got here?
Old sweatsocks	End of the breakwater	HHI	
Fishing lure	Turquoise Beach		Left behind by swimmers?
		I	Fell off a boat

Top 5 beach trash items

1. Cigarette butts: 2 million
2. Caps and lids: 1.2 million
3. Plastic bottles: 1.1 million
4. Plastic bags: 1 million
5. Food containers: 900,000

Singing Stones

The shore's perfect for a little rock music.

Beach and river stones are time-honored music-makers. People have played them as percussion instruments for thousands of years, and even today we love the tone of a fine *lithophone* (an instrument whose keys are made of rock). The quality of the song, though, depends on the quality of the stone.

Search out flat, oval rocks, like those you'd use for skipping stones. Rocks with long, straight molecules, such as flint, granite, and slate (which are often smooth and dark, and are commonly found on lake and creek shores), resonate clearly, but you can experiment with any type of rock.

Knock stones together hard and soft, fast and slow. Cup a stone in your palm and tap another against it, opening and closing your fingers to alter the sound's pitch. Scratch them together, or click them castanet-style. Then wet down your stones and play them again. Does the tone grow richer?

Science Meets Art: Jim Denevan

Sand, water, and ice are this artist's canvas, and the huge abstract pictures he draws on them are eventually erased by waves and weather. Sometimes he makes "spirographs" on beach and lake sands, using GPS to get his mile-wide circles just right. Or he uses a rake to carve vast spirals best viewed from seagull height.

Making such big art requires both exploration—"I'm sure I've walked around the world a couple of times in the sand," Denevan says—and close attention to the landscape. Though his work is precise and takes lots of effort, he likes the fact that nature will eventually mess it up. "The ocean and the weather outdoors are much, much more powerful than any grand composition.... I love it when it washes away."

Experiment with sand drawing on your shoreline. Use sticks or your hands to draw patterns or pictures, or build a fancy sand castle. Return in a few hours—or a few days. Is your work still there? What has the wind and water taken away, or added to it?

LAB #12

Game Hour

What to do in the free hour between homework and dinner? Get your friends over and get your game on with awesome illusions, contests, and even a roller coaster ride.

What makes toys roll and move? One way to find out: Open them up!

Scratch up some old songs—no software or stereo required.

Bring flat stuff to 3-D life with colored filters!

Race robotic insects through the house!

No need for a costume party—just slap on a handmade mask and scare them silly.

Turn your sofa and chairs into a roller-coaster track.

Tangle up your eyes with crazy optical illusions.

3-Do It!

What brings a dead monster to life? 3-D magic, cooked up when your eyes take in two different images of the same beast. Your brain blends them into a single pic that leaps off the page.

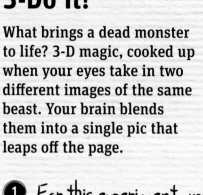

1 For this experiment, you'll need to buy clear red and blue acetate sheets at a crafts-supply store. Once you're back at home, draw a line with a few shades of blue pencils, then choose the color whose line vanishes when you look at it through the blue sheet. Do the same with the red sheet and a few shades of red pencils. (Crayons work well, too.)

2 Put the tips of the pencils on the monster below, and follow its outline with both pencils at once. Get its details—such as the fierce teeth—too! Or try this on a black-and-white drawing that you create yourself.

3 Cut the acetate sheets into small squares that can cover your eyes. Hold the red sheet over one eye and the blue sheet over the other, and watch the monster roar to life!

The Three Little Pig(ment)s

Shadows aren't always black. Colored ones are extra fun!

1 This game requires you, two friends, three flashlights (with bright bulbs for maximum effect), and three clear acetate sheets in red, blue, and green. Tape a different colored acetate sheet to each person's flashlight head.

2 Kill the room lights. Line up in front of a white wall, with the green flashlight in the middle, the red one to the right, and the blue one to the left. The person with the green light aims it straight at the wall; the blue and red flashlight-wielders slant their lights so they hit the same area as the green light.

3 Hold your free hands between the flashlights and the wall. How many shadows do you see? What color are they? Move your hands to overlap their shadows and watch which hues appear in the overlapped areas. Now block one flashlight. What happens to the colored shadows? As you experiment, count all the colors you can make. Can you combine your beams to make white light, too?

What's the Deal?

You've already learned that white light contains all the colors of the rainbow. But here you combine three colors of light—green, red, and blue—to make white light as well as four other hues: cyan, magenta, yellow, and black. When your hand blocks one light beam, it doesn't cast a black shadow, but one filled with a mix of the other two flashlights' colors. Blue plus green makes a cyan shadow. Red plus blue makes magenta; red plus green makes yellow. When you overlap shadows, you block two beams, and blue, red, or green shadows emerge. And when you block all three beams, the shadows go black.

The Handprint Illusion

Turn a 2-D handprint into a crazy-colorful optical illusion!

① Lay your hand flat on a piece of white paper. Trace it, outstretched fingers and all, in pencil.

② Using markers, draw horizontal lines across the paper from left to right—but when you reach your hand's outline, curve the marker's line slightly upward from the left edge of the outline to its right edge. Then continue with a straight line to the paper's far edge.

③ Make lines in new colors until the whole paper's filled up. Don't forget to curve the lines inside your fingers' outlines! When you're done, you'll swear a 3-D hand is pushing outward from the paper's surface.

Mastered the hand? Try complex objects such as castles, people, animals, and trees, penciling their outlines first and then using the markers as explained above.

Science Meets Art: Edgar Müller

In his massive 3-D street-art illusions, Müller is a master of *trompe l'oeil:* a technique that tricks our sensory systems into believing that flat images have dimension, weight, and especially depth. On this completely solid and ordinary Irish pier, the artist sketched the outlines of a huge crevasse and painted its surface in blue, gray, and white. In the end, a titanic glacial gap seemed to split the pier apart—an effect so realistic that some passersby refused to walk over the dizzying illusion. Müller explains that he likes to question the "daily perceptions of people by changing the appearance of public places"— in other projects, he has turned a Canadian roadway into a rushing waterfall and made mysterious trees erupt out of Danish streets.

Gather pens, paints, and paper—by playing with perspective and color, can you create art that seems to rip open the flat surfaces of daily life?

The Ames Trapezoid

An Ames "window" is a *trapezoid* (a rectangle taller on one side than the opposite side). But our eyes and brain think it's a regular rectangle seen from an angle, producing a gotta-see-it-to-believe-it illusion.

You'll need:
2 sheets of paper
Glue
Cardboard
Craft knife
Hole puncher and scissors
Lightweight thread
Double-sided foam tape
3-inch- (7.5-cm-) long piece of craft stick, or a toothpick

1 Photocopy the template here on two sheets of paper. Glue one sheet to each side of a piece of cardboard, carefully aligning them. Now cut out the double-sided window with the craft knife, and trim out its panes. You have an ordinary-looking window frame with six empty panes.

2 Use the hole puncher to make a hole in each upper corner of the frame. Cut a 2-foot- (60-cm-) long piece of thread, and knot one end in each of these holes. Hang the thread off one finger so the window is evenly balanced, and, with your free hand, turn the window a few times so the thread twists.

3 Raise the window to eye level and let the thread untwist. The window rotates as the thread unwinds, but something odd happens, too. You don't see the window turn—it seems to *oscillate* (move) from side to side.

4 Lower the window below eye level. Now you can clearly see that the window's turning through 360-degree rotations. Raise it back to eye level, and it oscillates again.

Put a small strip of double-sided tape inside a top "windowpane," then press the craft stick or toothpick through the pane and onto the tape. Now spin the window at eye level as you did before. The stick turns in regular circles, but the window still oscillates—so the stick seems to magically zip through the frame!

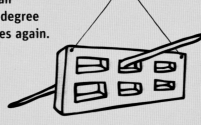

Illusions tease our eyes and show scientists how our brains see the world.

Make a Miniature Roller Coaster

Rig up a roller coaster to see how you can use the laws of physics to create thrilling hills and loops.

1 **Vertically cut** 12 feet (3.7 m) of pool noodles or thick foam-pipe insulation (from a hardware store) into half-pipes of varied lengths. These are the coaster tracks. Duct-tape sections together, smoothing out wrinkles so your "cars"— a handful of marbles—can roll swiftly.

2 **First make** a *big* hill: Tape a half-pipe to a tall support. Tape its end to another half-pipe resting on a lower support, then tape that one's end to a lower prop. Ask a friend to roll a marble down the first hill. It should fly smoothly and quickly.

3 **Make more hills,** set on chairs or other sturdy stuff. Test each with a marble roll. If the marble slides backward, stop to redesign. Pointer: Each hill must be shorter than the one before it.

What's the Deal?

The marble races in some spots but moseys along in others. Why? Gravity gets the marble going, and once it zooms up a hill, it's filled with *potential energy.* That turns into *kinetic energy* as it zips down the far side. But when it treks up the next hill, some kinetic energy turns back into potential energy, and some is lost as friction. So each time a marble goes up a hill, more kinetic energy is lost, making your marble a little less powerful. That's why your first hill—like the first rise in a real coaster—must be the tallest: The marble wouldn't have enough energy to climb a taller hill later on.

4 **Got your coasting mojo down?** Build a loop after a super-high hill. Try out a circle, then an oval-shaped loop, to see which works best—you might be surprised by the answer.

Does a curve or a straightaway before help or hinder your marble? Try both, fine-tune the track for maximum vroom

The Robobug

Slap together these rad runarounds with a friend, then see whose 'bot can crawl across the room fastest—or make the cat jump highest.

You'll need:
Several little brushes
(toothbrushes and small scrubbers work well)
Scissors
Pliers
Double-sided foam tape
Small vibrating DC electrical motors,
one per brush, 1 to 10 volts*
Rubber bands
Watch batteries, one per brush, 1.5 to 3 volts
Superglue
Colored felt
Stick-on googly eyes
Pipe cleaners, feathers, and other decorations
Clear tape

* Order these online, or dig them out of old cell phones and toys with an adult's help.

1 Salvage old brushes from the kitchen, bathroom, or garage. Check that their bristles are even. If they're not, trim them with scissors so they'll run smoothly. If you're using a toothbrush, carefully break or snip off the head with pliers, asking an adult for help.

2 Turn the brushes bristle side down and put a strip of double-sided foam tape on each one's back.

3 Choose your motor: A big scrub brush needs a motor with high voltage, but a toothbrush head needs a lower-voltage one. Secure your motor and battery to the brush using tape or rubber bands, sandwiching one of the motor's wires between the tape and the battery.

Pipe cleaners

Feathers

Rubber band

Large vibrating electrical motor

Small vibrating electrical motor

Watch battery

Foam tape

Brush head

4 Now decorate your critter. Glue felt around the brush head for "tentacles," stick on googly eyes, make antennae and legs from pipe cleaners, and glue on feathers for a rooster tail.

5 Press the motor's free wire to the top side of the battery, secure it with a bit of clear tape, and watch your critter come to life, vibrating and wiggling across the floor.

Mask-o-Morphosis

Humans have made masks for millennia to scare, be silly, and play at being other people, animals, or gods. Transform yourself and your friends with a game exploring why masks are so powerful.

1 **Pick the feelings** or characters that your masks will show: ferocious or shy? Funny or sad? Create your masks from paper bags, string, colored paper, paint, and anything else you can stick on your head.

2 **Put on a mask,** and then try to make your body match your mask. How does a scary body move? And how does your posture change when you're sad?

3 **Play around:** Can you make little gestures show big emotions? Does hiding your face make moving in new or odd ways easy? Why?

4 **Try to work** against your mask. Can you turn a cute character into a fearsome one? Or transform a terrifying creature into a goofy one?

Move Groove

Dig out your folks' old LPs and spin some vinyl. No record player? No problem!

1 **Pick an LP** without warps or scratches, and get your parents' thumbs-up to play with it. Slide a pencil through its hole, then wrap tape around the pencil below the record so it can't slide out.

2 **Roll a big piece of paper** into an ice-cream-cone shape and tape its edges together. Stick a straight pin in it just below the tip—pin head inside the cone, pin tip outside it. Voilà: a sound arm and needle!

3 **Now let's rock.** Hold the LP and pencil with the point up and the eraser end down. Hold the cone so the pin's point sits in a groove near the LP's outer edge.

4 **Ask a friend** to rotate the LP. As the pin moves in the groove, it hits tiny bumps and bends that make the pin and c[ ] vibrate and create sound waves. The sound improves as you speed up the LP's spin—the faster you go, the clearer the sou[ ]

104

The Toy Take-Apart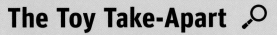

Dust off the old toys at the back of the closet, raid the toolbox, and investigate the mechanics that make these things run.

1 **Gather a "dissection" kit:** small screwdrivers, needlenose pliers, tweezers, and this book's magnifier. Slip on safety glasses.

2 **Pick out toys** to sacrifice to science: tops, pull-back racing cars, and windup dolls are perfect subjects. Choose ones with visible screws or joints, not ones that are single pieces of molded plastic or metal (those are hard to open) or that plug into walls (those can hold some electrical charge).

3 **First remove** any batteries, then undo the toy's screws and pins, spreading them out as you work. Now pull the toy apart segment by segment. What's inside? Circuit boards, light bulbs, and wires? Springs and rubber bands?

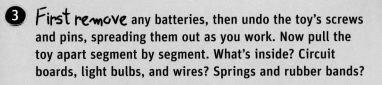

Many modern toys hold a microchip. Clip its attached wires and lift it out. Some hold voice samples, as in those teddy bears that coo, "I wuv you!" Some control motion, as in toy trains that steer away from obstacles. What do you think your toy's chip does?

In a windup toy, you'll see a plastic gearbox attached to a knob or a key that sticks out of the toy. Pry it open to see the gears and spring within: These power pins and shafts in the toy's wheels or limbs make it move. Can you find the gears' attachment point to your toy's moving parts?

After you've dissected each toy, invent fresh uses for its parts. Create mechanical mischief by stripping wires and taping them to new places to make a car's headlights moo or a cow light up. Or design a unique stuffed animal by sewing a teddy bear back together inside out or attaching another toy's limbs to it.

USAF

UNITED STATES OF AMERICA

USAF

LAB #13

Marvelous Mealtime

Eating with the folks tonight? Use everything in the kitchen, from the cookware to the meal on your plate, to sink your teeth into the secrets of food.

Flower vase or self-portrait... or both?

One cupcake's yucky, one's yummy. Why?

Mummify your meal!

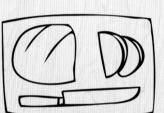

The tastiest bread is made with...farts!

Amplify your voice with a cooking pan.

)))

Turn pickles into power dynamos.

Hey, who invited the bacteria to dinner?

Transform dull old table salt into crazy artworks.

Face Vase!

Kid or flowerpot? It's the viewer's call in this figure-ground illusion investigation.

① **Look at the photo here.** Can you see a blue vase-like shape between the girl's two profiles? Can you focus on the profiles and the vase at the same time?

② **Now make** your own illusion. Sit sideways in a chair before a white wall. Ask a relative to set a lamp so light falls on your profile. Tape a white paper sheet to the wall, then sit so your silhouette fits on the sheet.

③ **Ask your relative** to trace your silhouette on the paper. Take it off the wall, stack it with a plain sheet of white paper, and cut out your silhouette from both sheets. Leave the straight sides alone.

④ **Tape a white face** to the edge of a sheet of dark paper, nose inward. Flip the other white face and tape it to the other edge so the noses are even and 1 inch (2.5 cm) apart. Can you see the vase and faces at once? Nope—your eyes can take in only one element at a time.

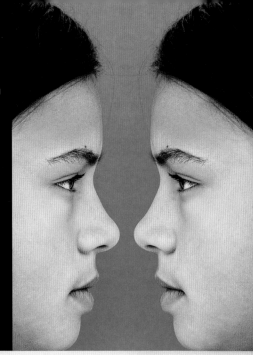

Sugar Rainbow Stir-'Em-Ups

Why not start your dinner with a rainbow? This brilliantly striped experiment adds color to your table and teaches you about mass, volume, and density, too.

❶ **Turn the faucet** to hot. Collect ½ cup (120 mL) hot water and pour it in a ceramic cup. Do the same with three more cups.

❷ **Add 8 tablespoons** (120 g) of sugar to the first cup. Stir in several drops of blue food coloring until it and the sugar have dissolved.

❸ **Add 6 tablespoons** (90 g) of sugar and green food coloring to the second cup and mix. Repeat—with 4 tablespoons (60 g) of sugar plus yellow, then 2 tablespoons (30 g) of sugar plus red—in the third and the fourth cups.

❹ **Give all four cups time** to cool down. Now hold a tall, skinny glass at an angle. With an eyedropper, carefully drip the colored sugar waters, one at a time, into the glass, working in this order: blue, green, yellow, and red.

What's the Deal?

Do the colors mix together? No—they stay in their pretty layers because of a dandy math formula: *Mass* (the number and size of the atoms in a substance) divided by *volume* (how much space the substance takes up) = *density*. When you add more sugar to the same amount of water, the solution grows denser. The sweetest water sinks to the bottom, and the lightest sits on top.

Crumble Cracker Continents

Investigate the titanic forces shaking Earth's continents—just by playing with snack crackers. Geology class was never so sweet.

1 **Choose crackers** with perforations, like grahams. Snap one in half on a dotted line—your "fault line"—and push the pieces together until they touch. Shift one away from yourself, one toward yourself.

2 **Crumbs fall off** as the pieces scrape together, just as when two continental plates scrape past each other on a *strike-slip fault line*, shedding rock and causing quakes.

3 **Snap one piece** into two smaller halves with an uneven break, and then scrape their edges up and down against each other. The pieces build up stress, just as continental plates do along a *reverse fault*. At last the pieces will snap, just as plates do in a big quake.

4 **Move one piece** under another to see what happens when a continental plate dives under a second plate and forces it up (a process called *subduction*). More crumbs fall off the cracker, and one piece might shatter. When this happens quickly on a geologic scale, huge temblors, such as the Indian Ocean undersea *megathrust quake* of 2004, can wreak widespread havoc.

Wok Talk

Before you sauté veggies, use a wok—or any big, curved metal bowl—to amp up your voice.

1 **Hold the wok** by its handles, bowl side to your face. Warble, talk, or babble while slowly moving the wok to your mouth.

2 **Stop when your voice** grows louder: You've found the *focal point*, where sound waves from your lips bounce cleanly off the metal back to your ears.

3 **Now talk, talk, talk** to the back of the wok. Sound waves bounce off the bottom and spread all over the place—and someone might holler at you to keep it down.

Bottle Boogie

Build yourself an old-fashioned big glass band right out of the recycling bin.

① **Find four identical glass bottles.**
Or, if you'd like a full octave (meaning the basic group of musical notes, C–D–E–F–G–A–B–C), use eight bottles.

② **Use a measuring cup**
with a spout to pour different amounts of water into each one.

③ **Tap each bottle** with a spoon, pencil, or chopstick, then line up your bottles by lowest to highest sound.

④ **Blow across each bottle's top** to make it hoot. Now which one is lowest and which one's highest? Re-sort your bottle lineup accordingly.

What's the Deal?

When you tap on a bottle, you make it vibrate, which produces sound. The *pitch* of that sound—whether it's high or low—depends on how much water is in the bottle. A lot of water means slow vibration and a low pitch. And a little water means fast vibration and a high pitch. But when you blow on a bottle, you make the *air* inside it (not the bottle itself) vibrate—and this changes everything! More water now equals less air, which results in fast vibration and a high pitch. And less water means more air—causing slow vibration and low pitch.

Have eight bottles? Sort them into a scale so you can play real tunes! Fill the first with ¼ inch (6.5 mm) of water, and the next with ½ inch (1.25 cm). Proceed along the next six, adding ¼ inch (6.5 mm) more water to each one than you did to the last. Now find a toy electronic keyboard or listen to an online musical clip of an octave. Adjust the amount of water in each bottle until the band's in perfect tune!

Bake Fake Cupcakes

These look delicious but taste despicable. Making them tells you a lot about why ingredients play well together—or don't—in our food.

Bowl 1
2 tsp (10 mL) Vaseline
½ tsp (2.5 mL) liquid soap
1 Tbsp (15 mL) vanilla

Special ingredients

Bowl 2
2 tsp (10 mL) Vaseline
1 Tbsp (15 mL) beaten egg
1 Tbsp (15 mL) vanilla

Bowl 3
2 tsp (10 mL) butter
1 Tbsp (15 mL) beaten egg
1 Tbsp (15 mL) vanilla

1 **Preheat the oven** to 375°F (190°C). Mark two liners with #1, two with #2, and two with #3. Put each set into the cupcake pan.

2 **Mix all dry ingredients** (shown below) in the big bowl.

2 cups (473 g) flour

1½ cups (355 g) sugar

2 tsp (10 g) cinnamon

1 tsp (5 g) ground cloves

Sculpt Salt Stalactites

Turn the plainest item on your table into a colorful work of art.

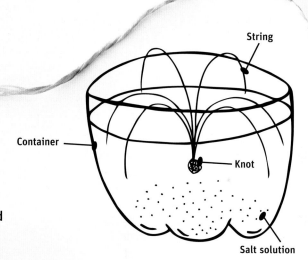

String

Container

Knot

Salt solution

1 **Cut six or seven** 5-inch- (13-cm-) long pieces of white string, and knot them at one end into a string "bouquet."

2 **Bring 1 cup** (237 mL) of water to a boil in a saucepan and stir in ¼ cup (59 g) of table salt a bit at a time until it's all dissolved. Then mix in a full bottle of food coloring. Flick off the heat, let the solution cool a bit, and pour it into a sturdy plastic cup (try the sliced-off butt of a liter soda bottle).

3 Mix the special ingredients (see the lists opposite) in each of the three medium bowls. Divide the dry mixture evenly among the bowls and stir.

¾ cup (180 mL) ginger ale

You'll need:
6 paper cupcake liners
Pen and paper
Cupcake pan
1 big bowl
3 medium bowls
Ingredients shown at left

4 Add ¼ cup (60 mL) of ginger ale to each bowl and stir.

5 Pour bowl 1 into the liners marked 1, bowl 2 into the liners marked 2, and so on. Write down which set of liners holds each bowl's contents. Bake for 30 minutes or until an inserted toothpick comes out clean.

6 Compare the taste, smell, and texture of each set of cupcakes. Yum? Blech? Which are tastiest? Which taste the worst? (Eat only a bit of each type! Soap and Vaseline could upset your stomach if you take more than a bite.)

What's the Deal?

A cake's basic ingredients are water and flour. But if you use only those, you wind up with a gray rock. So recipes include a *lubricant* (butter or oil) and a *foaming agent* (baking powder) to make the treat tender and fluffy. Eggs are *emulsifiers*, which make other ingredients mix together well, and sugar and spices are tasty extras. In these not-so-nice cakes, you used all these basics, but wacko versions of them—Vaseline as lubricant, ginger ale as foaming agent, and soap as emulsifier. All the variants made nice-looking cupcakes. But only some of them are edible!

3 Stick the knotted end of your strings in the solution. Flop the loose ends evenly around the container's rim like octopus arms.

4 Leave your project in a quiet place for two days while salt crystals creep up the strings. Make more colored salt solution to pour in so the salt stalactites will grow thicker.

5 After a couple of days, take the strings out of the solution and set them aside. Repeat the steps above, using fresh strings and a new color. Do this several times, then arrange all the results into a wild-looking Salt Beast to display on the dinner table.

What's the Deal?

When you stir salt into water, its crystals dissolve and it goes into *solution*. But you can't dissolve an infinite amount of salt in a fixed amount of water. When as much salt has dissolved as possible, the salt solution becomes *saturated*. If more salt is added, it's then *supersaturated*, and salt grains will settle at the container's bottom. But hot water holds more dissolved salt than cold water can because it has more kinetic energy. When your solution cools down, the salt crystallizes back into solid form, grabbing onto the porous strings and drying there in scaly formations.

Your Dear Old Mummy

You don't have a corpse lying around, so open the fridge, grab a hot dog, and turn it into your own personal mummy. Curses optional.

1 *Ancient Egyptians* mummified mostly famous folks, so pick a royal name for your hot dog. Set Empress Pupemhotep on a kitchen scale to get her weight. Use a ruler to measure her length, and a 3-inch- (7.5-cm-) long string to measure her diameter. Record the figures in a notebook.

2 *Fill a plastic box* a bit bigger than the hot dog with 2 inches (5 cm) of baking soda. Set the hot dog inside, cover it with 2 inches (5 cm) of baking soda, and put on the box's lid. Stick the box in a cabinet for a week. Unearth the hot dog, remeasure it, and record the stats.

3 *Repowder it,* store it for 10 more days, then dig it up and measure again. The baking soda has sucked out water and stopped *rot,* or bacterial growth, and the mummy is now yours for eternity.

What's the Deal?

The ancient Egyptians employed a naturally occurring salt from the Nile, *natron,* to preserve their dead. It is composed of dehydrating sodium carbonate, sodium bicarbonate (which is baking soda), sodium sulfate, and sodium chloride (table salt). First they scooped out a corpse's guts, except for its heart (they left that for the gods to weigh to see if the person had led a good life), and filled the body with natron or linen cloth. Then came a coat of more natron. The stuffing soaked up internal juices, the natron slurped up the rest, and then the remains were wrapped in linen, buried, and left to inspire generations of future archaeologists.

Feast on Farts!

Pick up a slice of bread and eyeball that thing. It's full of tiny holes. What makes 'em? Farts! Yeast farts, to be precise. See for yourself with this gassy gastronome's test.

1 *Blow up* a medium rubber balloon a few times so that it's nice and stretchy.

2 *Stir two packets* of active dry baker's yeast and 4 tablespoons (57 g) of sugar into 1 cup (237 mL) of warm water (105 to 115°F/40–46°C).

3 *Pour this brew* into a clean 1-L glass bottle. Stretch the balloon's opening over the bottle's mouth so it's airtight.

4 *The water will bubble* as the yeasties eat the sugar and emit carbon dioxide. (Our farts are a little different from yeast farts, by the way—we emit carbon dioxide, too, but we also blast out oxygen, nitrogen, methane, hydrogen, and hydrogen sulfide.)

5 *After a few minutes,* the balloon will rise and fill up with yeast farts. That's exactly how yeast—known as *leavening*—makes stretchy dough rise when you're baking bread. Yum!

Power Up Pickles

Salty, snappy, a sandwich's best friend—
and a source of hidden superpower!

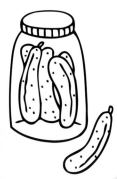

1 **At a hobbyist shop,** buy two little alligator-clip leads and a low-voltage DC piezo buzzer. Look at the label to make sure the buzzer carries only about 10mA (milliamperes) of current.

2 **Back at home,** fork a fat pickle out of the jar in the fridge. Carefully cut a 1-inch- (2.5-cm-) long slit in it with a paring knife. Insert a copper coin into the slit.

3 **Close to the copper coin,** firmly stick a #6 or #8 galvanized nail into the pickle.

4 **With an alligator-clip lead,** connect the buzzer's positive terminal to the copper coin. With the other clip, attach the buzzer's negative terminal to the nail. *Buzz!* You've turned your pickle into a battery!

What's the Deal?

Pickles contain saltwater, and that's rich in *ions*—charged particles. The copper coin and the zinc nail react with the ions and start an electrical tug-of-war. The copper has more power, so it pulls electrons away from the nail. That sets electrons flowing in a current around the circuit, powering the buzzer. Ordinary batteries work the same way, minus the dill: They use two metals in ion-rich liquid to separate electrical charge and thus create a current. (But they taste lousy with pastrami on rye.)

You'll need:

Two alligator-clip leads
Low-voltage (6–16 -volt)
DC piezo buzzer
Extra-large kosher dill pickle
Copper coin
#6 or #8 galvanized
nail

Piezo buzzer

Buzzer's positive lead

Buzzer's negative lead

Copper coin

Galvanized nail

Alligator clip connected to buzzer's positive lead

Alligator clip connected to buzzer's negative lead

Join the Bug-Eating Brigade!

Insects are nutritious, delicious, and enjoyed the world over. Explore *entomophagy* by sampling one of these wriggles—all of them high in protein and fiber, low in fat, and tasty as can be.

Bon daegi (Korea)

Buy crispy centipede kebabs at Chinese market stalls, or make them at home: Skewer them lengthwise (add veggies if you like), brush them with olive oil, and cook them over a grill for a few minutes.

Centipedes (China)

Sizzle *bon daegi* (silkworm larvae) in hot oil like popcorn, then dust with rock salt. Witchetty grubs, moth larvae adored by Australia's Aboriginal peoples, are chewed raw or roasted in the hot coals of a campfire.

Witchetty grubs (Australia)

**Scorpions
(Southeast Asia)**

To cook a scorpion, stab it behind the head, cut off its stinger, and skewer it. Roast it until it's brown and crisp, then eat it in one bite. Fried tarantulas taste a little like crab—start with the crackly legs, then savor the gooey, nut-flavored abdomen.

**Chapulines
(Mexico)**

**Tarantulas
(Cambodia)**

If you score some *chapulines* (grasshoppers) in a Mexican specialty market, wash them, deep-fry them, and season them with lime, salt, and chile. Pick off and discard their wings and legs, then relish these potato chip–like crunchies.

Science Meets Art:
The Garbage Geniuses

Way out on the foggy fringe of San Francisco, artists scavenge in heaps of trash in the city dump. What are they doing? They're making art! By giving artists raw materials, the dump inspires people to protect the land and promotes new ways to think about art and the environment.

This is no ordinary art: Tamara Albaitis makes sound sculptures out of abandoned stereo speakers, wire, and salvaged CDs. Old drills, saws, motors, and gears compose Nemo Gould's sculptures (at right). And Amy Wilson Faville transforms old furniture, toys, and clothing people dump on sidewalks into haunting paintings.

The next time you take out the trash, think of the stuff in the can as material for your own creations. Could that ripped-up cardboard become a sculpture? What if you arranged and painted all those empty soup cans? Let your imagination fly: Throwaways are trash only if we think they're trash. But if you believe they can be art, they will be!

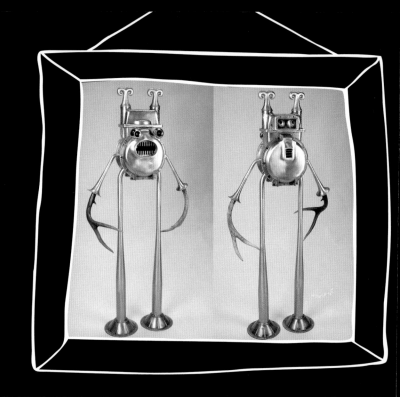

Feed Me!

After you eat your own dinner, it's time to feed your garden. The snack it likes best? A rich homemade compost pile cooked up in the backyard.

You'll need:
Prefab compost bin (from a garden store)
Brown material (dead leaves, newspaper)
Green vegetation (grass clippings, foliage)
Yard soil

① Follow the rule of thirds: Layer one-third brown material (which is rich in carbon), one-third green vegetation (rich in nitrogen), and one-third soil (which provides microbes and worms that start the compost "cooking").

② Later, almost anything goes: meal leftovers, dead plants, coffee grounds, even dryer lint and pet hair. Go for a 25:1 ratio of brown stuff to green stuff. Don't add weeds—they'll sprout in the pile.

③ Add cow, horse, or chicken poop for extra nutrients (steer clear of pet and human waste, bones, and meat scraps to prevent rat hordes out back).

④ Sprinkle the heap with water sometimes so it stays as damp as a moist sponge. Turn the heap often to get air into it, or it'll stink. The goal: a rich, earthy smell—and a crumbly brown look—that says the compost is ready for you to add to your veggie patches and flowerbeds.

Yard soil
Green vegetation
Brown material

What Lurks Behind the Can? 🔍

When you're washing the dishes, consider this: All over your kitchen, colonies of bacteria are growing. Time to discover just what's living in your home's grubby corners.

You'll need:
Packet of agar
(from a health-food store)
Water
Saucepan
Sugar
Clean, shallow glass bowl
Plastic wrap
Clear tape

1 Empty the agar and 1 cup (240 mL) of water into a saucepan. Bring it to a boil. Turn it off and stir in 1 teaspoon (5 g) of sugar.

2 Pour the mixture into the glass bowl and cover it with plastic wrap so no bacteria bumble in yet. Let it cool to a smooshy gel: ideal microbe food.

3 Now find a grimy, slimy, moist area of the kitchen. Behind the trash can? The floor near the dog's dish? Oh, yeah!

4 Stick a piece of tape on the surface and pull it up several times. Rush back to your agar bowl.

5 Lift off the plastic wrap, press the tape's sticky side on the gel, remove the tape, and re-cover the bowl.

6 Store your dish on a cool, dark shelf. Come back in a week to see fuzzy colonies of fungi and bacteria spreading on the gel. Inspect them with the magnifier from this book—pretty, aren't they? Now go scrub the floor.

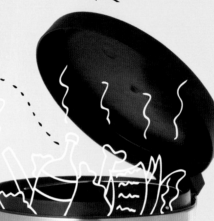

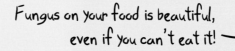
Fungus on your food is beautiful, even if you can't eat it! →

Penicillium roqueforti on blue cheese

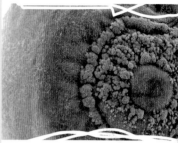
Monilia fructigena on a peach

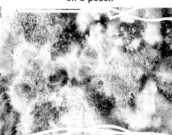
Rhizopus nigricans mold on bread

Rhizopus stolonifer mold on tomato

Penicillium and *Aspergillus* molds on lemon

Nighty-Night!

Before you draw the blankets over your day, investigate the spooky secrets of the dark side of life—from starshine to moonbeams to dreamtime.

You want to go to outer space and you want to get there NOW—but which vehicle's the fastest?

To see these eyes really glow, carry this book outside into the night!

Chirp! Chirp!

Check the temperature with crickets, nature's own thermometers.

At sunset, figure out the secret of the legendary green flash.

Dream of space travel with a stomp-powered sky flier.

The Man in the Moon's not the only one living in here.

What's that scurrying across the sky? A comet, a UFO, or a satellite?

Play Ping-Pong with the full Moon—and figure out the finest nights for Moon-watching.

Why do we snore? To scare away the tigers!

Can you craft a light bulb that doesn't use a lamp or even a socket?

Make a DIY telescope from recycling-bin bits to investigate the heavens.

What's That in the Bushes!?

Spooked by yellow eyes glaring from the bushes? Learn which critters' eyes glow at night—and why.

1. **First round up your dog or cat.** Bring it into a dark room. Then lasso a friend or relative, and bring him in there, too.

2. **Briefly shine** a flashlight in their eyes from 6 feet (1.8 m) away. Your brother's eyes won't light up, but your pet's eyes will look bright green or yellow. Rowr.

What's the Deal?

The eyes of cats—as well as deer, dogs, horses, and alligators, among others—hold a layer of light-reflective cells, the *tapetum lucidum* (Latin for "luminous carpet"). It gives animals great night vision because their eyes can detect light both when it enters the pupil and again when light reflects inside the eye.

The Light Bulb Puzzle

Make the night glow with a light bulb that you don't have to stick in a lamp or even plug into a socket.

Your goal: Build a structure that gets electric current from one of the flashlight bulb's *terminals* through its *filament* and back to the other terminal so the bulb will light up. (The filament is the little wire inside the bulb. The terminals are the tiny dent and bump on the bulb's base.)

Tape the lightweight wire to the terminals and the D battery in various ways. Some structures will get that filament glowing. Others won't.

There's no single answer—keep your scientist's hat on and your curiosity sharp, and you'll discover several tricks that light up the night.

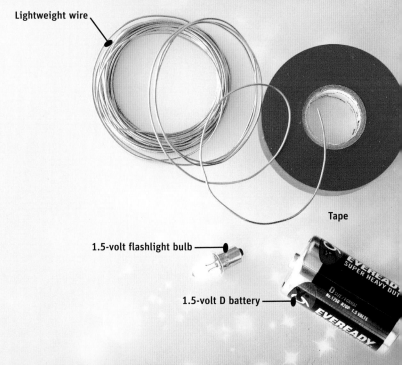

Lightweight wire

Tape

1.5-volt flashlight bulb

1.5-volt D battery

The Six-Legged Thermometer

Can an insect tell you whether to put on a sweater? Sure can—if it's a cricket.

1 **Sit outside and listen** for a loud cricket. These cold-blooded guys chirp fast in warm weather, when they're looking to mate, and slow in cool weather.

2 **To estimate the temperature** in Fahrenheit, count the chirps you hear in 14 seconds. Add 40. The result will be within spitting distance of a thermometer's reading.

3 **For Celsius,** count chirps for 25 seconds. Divide the count by 3, then add 4 to get the temperature. (Note: If it's very cold, these calculations won't work—the crickets are too cold for romance.)

There's a myth that crickets can sense approaching rainstorms and burrow underground beforehand. But crickets themselves would disagree: An insect that buried itself in the dirt could drown in a downpour.

Glimpse the Green Flash

Here's a rare sunset sight that a lucky few may spot: As the Sun dips below the horizon, a brilliant green flash flares for a moment, then vanishes. Is it an alien invasion? No, it's a *mirage*. When you watch a sunset, the Sun itself has already slipped below the horizon. But Earth's atmosphere bends its light upward, so we see a red-orange mirage of the Sun's disk. The atmosphere also scatters the light, treating each color of the rainbow differently, much as a glass prism does. So, as Earth rotates, the red, orange, and yellow hues disappear first; then go the green, blue, indigo, and violet. But on a clear night on an unobstructed horizon such as the sea, a green mirage might briefly appear. We don't usually see blue or violet flashes, because even a little haze knocks out those colors. All that's left is the strange, glowing emerald

Hunt Down the Full Moon

Want to know when the next full moon will appear? Make a Moon journal!

Check three things online before you start:

☐ The weather forecast, because you need two weeks of pretty clear skies.

☐ The time of sunset each evening—do your lunar look-see just afterward.

☐ The next new moon's date. New moons are invisible because they are on the same side of the Earth as the Sun. Start your journal a couple of nights later.

1 Draw 14 squares, one for every night you'll Moon-watch. Put a circle in each square, and leave space to write in the date.

2 The first night, a thin crescent moon will pop up in the west after sunset. Shade its crescent in your first circle. Where is it in the sky? Over your roof? By the water tower?

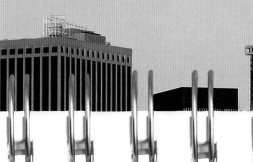

Aug. 26/over garage   Aug. 27/over driveway   Aug. 28/by chimney

3 Search for the Moon just after sunset for the next 13 nights. It'll be a different shape—and in a different place—each night. Draw it, and note where you see it. On the last evening, it will be a bright, round ball low in the eastern sky. Over the course of a month, moonrise happens 50 minutes later each day than it did the previous day. Because it rises later, the Moon rises in a slightly different place in the sky each night, too. New moons rise at sunrise and set at sunset. Full moons rise at sunset and set at sunrise.

Play Lunar Ping-Pong

Crescent, half, three-quarters, full—the Moon constantly changes shape, even though it's a sphere. Grab a Ping-Pong ball and you'll find out why.

Lamp

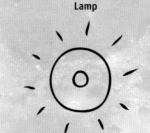

① You need a lamp and a room you can darken. Stick the lamp on a table at eye level. Take off its shade, flick it on, and turn off all other room lights.

② Turn your back to the lamp and hold the ball at eye level. Put a thumbtack in it as a "handle." Pretend that the lamp is the Sun, the ball is the Moon, and your own head is the Earth.

③ Now the ball looks like a full moon, bright and round. Face the ball and hold it steady as you slowly make a quarter turn counterclockwise. Now only half of the ball's lit-up area is visible to you, so it looks like a half-moon.

You

Ping-Pong ball

What's the Deal?

Half of your Ping-Pong ball is always lit by the lamp, just as half of the Moon is always lit by the Sun. And the same side of the ball is always facing you, just as the Moon keeps the same side facing Earth as it orbits us. But you can see only the lit-up section of the ball—likewise, from Earth, we see only the lit-up section of the Moon. The unlit part simply seems to vanish from view.

④ Keep moving in quarter-turns. As you turn toward the light, the ball will resemble a crescent moon.

Thumbtack

⑤ Move until the ball is between you and the light. The side that's facing you is dark, like a new moon.

⑥ Shuffle in a circle until your back is to the light, your Ping-Pong ball is bright again, and you've watched all the phases of your "Moon."

The Man (or the Frog or the Crab) in the Moon

Humans have told Moon myths ever since we first spotted that big white thing in the sky. After all, it's easy to "see" pictures in the Moon's cratered face. Here are a few Moon creatures from around the world.

MAN IN THE MOON
Europe, the Americas, and China, where he's called Yue-Laou, an old god of love.

RABBIT
Mesoamerica, East Asia, and the Southern Hemisphere. In Japan and Korea, it's grinding up ingredients for rice cakes.

FROG
Peru, Africa, and China. Angolan myth says the frog set up a prince's marriage to a Moon princess.

CRAB
South Pacific. In Melanesia, the crab is seen extending its claws from the Moon's north pole to its south pole.

Take a look—which creatures do you see? What stories could you create about them?

Ninja Vision!

Train yourself to see the invisible with this special spy's-eye trick.

On a clear, moonless night, far from city lights, look up and find a faint star. (Can you spot the Big Dipper? If so, peer at Alcor, the dimmest star in its handle.) Stare right at it. Now glance slightly above or below it—the star looks brighter! And if you search around, you'll find stars that you can see *only* when you are not looking directly at them.

When you stare at an object, its image falls on the *fovea*, a part of the eye full of photoreceptor cells called *cones* that work only in bright light. When you look a bit away from the object, its image falls on *rod* cells around the fovea. Rods need less light, so they send a stronger signal to the brain. Stargazers and stagehands—and others who sneak around in the dark—love this trick.

Chart Your Course to the Stars

Dreaming of a sky-high vacation? Choose your ride and your destination—and pack enough snacks for a *looong* trip.

MOON
(220,968 miles/355,614 km away)

MARS
(34 million miles/54.7 million km away)

	MOON	MARS
CAR (60 mph/ 97 kmh)	22 weeks	65 years
BULLET TRAIN (160 mph/ 258 kmh)	7 weeks, 2 days	21.7 years
PASSENGER JET (600 mph/ 966 kmh)	15 days	6.5 years
IMAGINARY STARSHIP (light speed)	1.2 seconds	3 minutes

Spy on Satellites

Around 24,500 man-made objects—operating satellites, dead ones, and random bits of junk—orbit the Earth every day. And some are easy to spot. On a clear, moonless night (check your Moon journal, on page 122), grab binoculars, tromp into the backyard, and give your eyes 10 minutes to adjust to the dark. Scan the sky for "stars" on the move. Found one? You just bagged a satellite! Some travel east-west; others (especially spy satellites) move north-south. You can even peek at the International Space Station: Check www.heavens-above.com to learn when it will flash through your skies.

And what happens to satellites once they die out and become space junk? Most space junk is too small for us to see, but it can harm spacecraft. We track large bits, but tiny ones aren't detectable. Cleanup ideas include nets and even orbiting garbage "trucks," but no one has found a solution yet.

SATURN
(741.2 million miles/1.2 billion km away)

PROXIMA CENTAURI
(4.3 light years away)

EPSILON ERIDANI
(10.3 light years away)

1,410 years	50 million years	110 million years
470 years	16.7 million years	36.7 million years
141 years	5 million years	11 million years
1 hour, 6 minutes	4.3 years	10.3 years

Trick Out a Telescope

Got a few supplies and a good pair of eyes? Then make yourself a 'scope and go stargazing.

1 Write down your lenses' *focal lengths,* which should be printed on their packaging. (Focal length is the distance, in millimeters, from a lens to the point where a telescope in which it's used is in focus.) The greater the difference between the two lenses, the stronger your telescope!

2 Cut the cardboard tube so it's as long as the longer of the two focal lengths. Wrap black construction paper around the cardboard tube, and tape it so it can slide up and down that tube. The paper tube must be longer than the shorter focal length.

3 Tape the lens with the longer focal length to one end of the cardboard tube. This is your *objective lens:* the one closest to the object you'll look at.

Turn your 'scope around to look through the objective lens. Gaze at something in the distance—it'll look smaller than it really is. Or look at an object close up, like your foot, through the objective lens. You'll get a magnified view...because your telescope is now a microscope!

4 Tape the lens with the shorter focal length to the far end of the construction-paper tube. This is your *eyepiece:* the thing you'll look through.

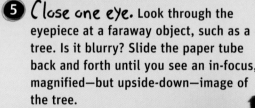

Lens with longer focal length

Cardboard tube

Construction paper tube

Tape

Tape

Lens with shorter focal length

You'll need:
Two convex lenses of different focal lengths (buy from online hobbyist shops)

Cardboard tube from a paper-towel roll

Scissors

Black construction paper

Clear tape

6 At night, turn your telescope to the sky and refocus. Can you spot faint stars or only the show-offs? (Yes, the image is still flipped, but that doesn't much matter when you're stargazing.)

5 Close one eye. Look through the eyepiece at a faraway object, such as a tree. Is it blurry? Slide the paper tube back and forth until you see an in-focus, magnified—but upside-down—image of the tree.

Science Meets Art: Don Pettit

This NASA astronaut's images—which are long-exposure photographs taken from the International Space Station—capture both starlight streaking into brilliant lines as Earth rotates and the blur of cities, thunderstorms, and the aurora borealis passing below him. Pettit creates multiple photos, keeping the shutter on his camera open for 30 seconds so Earth's rotation can smear light into long, colorful streaks.

Then he "stacks" the images on a computer so the lights' complete tracks are visible. On a clear night, you can create star-track photos from Earth's surface by putting a digital camera on a tripod, setting it for multiple half-minute exposures, and later putting the photos together in a photo-editing program. And one day, maybe you'll have the chance to shoot photos from space, too, just like Pettit.

Rig a Rocketship

It can't carry you to Jupiter, but this foot-fueled blaster is a guaranteed high flier.

You'll need:

2-L soda bottle

3 feet (90 cm) clear, flexible vinyl tubing with ½-inch (1.3-cm) interior diameter and ⅝-inch (1.6-cm) exterior diameter

Duct tape

2 feet (60 cm) PVC pipe with ½-inch (1.3-cm) interior diameter

Sheet of blank paper

Clear tape

3-by-5-inch (8-by-13-cm) index card

Scissors

A rocket-loving friend

1 Uncap the soda bottle and stick about 1 inch (2.5 cm) of vinyl tubing into it. Duct-tape the tubing in place—make sure the connection is airtight.

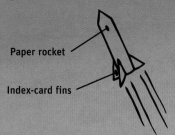

Paper rocket

Index-card fins

5 Now you gotta have rocket fins. Fold the index card in half. Cut along the fold line. Stack the halves and cut them diagonally, like a sandwich, to make four fins.

8 Three-two-one blastoff! Stomp on the bottle and watch that rocket soar.

2 Line up the PVC pipe with the tubing's free end. Duct-tape them together. Now you've got a rocket launcher!

6 Tape the fins evenly around the base of the paper rocket.

9 Now your pal gets a turn. Reinflate the bottle by blowing into the PVC tube.

3 Roll the paper around the PVC pipe in a tube loose enough to slide on and off. Tape the tube together and take it off the pipe.

PVC pipe

Duct tape

7 Call a friend to meet you outside. Put the rocket over the PVC tube, and ask him to hold the tube up but pointed away from your faces.

4 Twist one end of the paper tube into the rocket's "nose." Tape the twist in place and mash it until it's pointy.

Vinyl tubing

Duct tape

Soda bottle

The Jerk That Wakes You Up

Your stargazing is over, and it's time for sweet, sweet sleep. But suddenly, as you drift off, you're scared awake by a bizarre falling sensation. Yet you're still safe in bed, not tumbling down a dark well or sprawled on the floor. You're a victim of the *hypnic jerk!* These happen when your brain misreads signals from your sleepy, relaxing muscles as a loss of balance. It orders your limbs to get back to work, your leg or arm jerks in response, and *bam,* you're awake again. Some people have "dreamlets" of falling as this happens, or imagine they hear loud cracks or see brilliant lights. The strangest thing about the hypnic jerk? It's totally normal, and it happens to just about everyone.

Snoring for Survival

Your dad does it, your mom does it, and even you do it sometimes—that awful rattling, snorpling, snuffling thing called snoring. The physical reasons we do it are well known: Soft tissues in our nose and throat vibrate as they relax in sleep. But some scientists think snoring has another purpose: It makes us seem ferocious even when we're zonked out.

Consider an early human: dangerous when awake but harmless as dirt when he's asleep, and easy pickings for a predator hungry for a midnight snack. But then the predator hears thundering snorts and rumbles from the human's dark cave, grows nervous, and bolts away. Other scientists dismiss this theory, arguing that snoring would lead deadly beasts right to sleeping people—but it's just possible that our annoying snores helped us to survive the dangers of the primordial night.

weldonowen

President, CEO Terry Newell
VP, Sales Amy Kaneko
VP, Publisher Roger Shaw
Senior Editor Lucie Parker
Project Editor Laura Harger
Creative Director Kelly Booth
Art Director Meghan Hildebrand
Designer Michel Gadwa
Production Director Chris Hemesath
Production Manager Michelle Duggan

Weldon Owen is a division of **BONNIER**
Copyright © 2013 by the Exploratorium
and Weldon Owen Inc.
**All proceeds benefit the Exploratorium and
its programs.**

All rights reserved, including the right
of reproduction in whole or in part in
any form.

Library of Congress Control Number is
on file with the publisher.

ISBN 13: 978-1-61628-491-6
ISBN 10: 1-61628-491-9

10 9 8 7 6 5 4 3 2 1
2013 2014 2015 2016 2017
Printed in China by Toppan Excel.

Weldon Owen would like to thank the
Exploratorium for blowing our minds with
science throughout the creation of this book.
Special thanks go to rock-star educators Linda
Shore and Ken Finn for their invaluable help
in evaluating the book's science content. We'd
also like to thank Julie Nunn, Silva Raker,
Dana Goldberg, and Amy Snyder for their
enthusiasm, expertise, and assistance. The
Exploratorium also gratefully acknowledges
its Catalyst Circle Committee for its leadership
in resource development, which advances the
museum's educational mission.

Further gratitude is owed to Sarah Edelstein,
Iain Morris, Megan Peterson, and Noah
Potkin for design and production support;
Katharine Moore, Gail Nelson-Bonebrake, Katie
Schlossberg, and Marisa Solís for editorial
expertise; and David Bornfriend, Christian
Jusinski, and Stephen Lam for help on set.
Many thanks to Exalt Models and our kid
model crew: Faith, Kylie, Fiona, Cheyenne,
Taylor, Hannah, Bryce, Ludo, Jasper, DJ,
Adiahya, Ben, Kaylee, Noah, Daniel, and Jake.
Additional thanks to Carolyn Crimley, our
studio teacher.

15/17 Pier, San Francisco, CA 94111
www.exploratorium.edu

The Exploratorium—San Francisco's
renowned museum of science, art, and human
perception—is dedicated to changing the
way the world learns. The content in this
book began as exhibits, workshops, and
activities created through the Exploratorium's
educational and professional development
programs. These long-standing, highly
regarded programs include the Teacher
Institute, which supports secondary science
and math teachers; the Institute for Inquiry,
which offers workshops about the theory
and practice of inquiry; and the Community
Educational Engagement group, which provides
programs for children, youth, and families in
partnership with community organizations. For
more information, visit exploratorium.edu.

Exploratorium® is a registered trademark and
service mark of the Exploratorium.

Original photography by Erin Kunkel.
Prop styling by Peggi-Jane Jeung.
Original illustration by Jenna Rosenthal.

All additional photography from Shutterstock Images
unless noted below.

Cover: sky, bacteria, leaf, and water images all
courtesy of Amy Snyder.

pp. 10–11, all: Amy Snyder **pp. 12–13:** JR
Carvey/Streetfly/Getty Images **p. 20:** Brand X
Pictures/Getty Images **p. 23 (Elvis):** Ollie Atkins/
Wikicommons **p. 23 (Mona Lisa):** Wikicommons
p. 23 (bottom left): Julian Wolkenstein **p. 23 (faces
at far right, from top to bottom):** Martin Robertshaw,
Douglas Bauman, Joy Kidd, Dave Gorman, Kristen
Storm, Jan Schill, Amy Beth Geerling Payne **p. 27
(bottom, from left to right):** Nature Production,
Dr. Morely Read/Science Source, Peter Jackson
p. 28 (top): Richard Heeks **p. 28 (center left):** Tom
Falconer Photography **p. 29 (left):** Cultura Creative/
Alamy **p. 31 (fabric at far right, from top to bottom):**
David Becker, Andrew Coutts, David Becker, Brandon
Jones **p. 31 (bottom):** iStockphoto **p. 37 (right):**

Amy Snyder **pp. 38–39,** all: Inmagine.com **p. 45
(bottom right):** Andy Goldsworthy/Courtesy Galerie
Lelong, New York **p. 48:** Monashee Frantz/Getty
Images **p. 53 (bottom left):** Thomas Deerinck,
NCMIR/ScienceSource **p. 54 (top):** Judy Ulrick
p. 55 (right): Matt Shlian **pp. 56–57:** Floresco
Productions/Getty Images **p. 58 (left):** iStockphoto
p. 58 (right): Amy Snyder **p. 63 (far right):** Jessica
Hilltout; from *AMEN: Grassroots Football* **p. 64:**
Harri Tahvanainen/Getty Images **p. 67:** H. Cassea/
Corbis **p. 69 (bottom left):** *Nimbus II,* 2012; courtesy
Berndnaut Smilde and Ronchini Gallery; photo by
Cassander Eeftinck Schattenkerk **p. 69 (bottom
center):** H. Raab/Wikicommons **p. 69 (bottom right):**
iStockphoto **p. 70 (top):** John Lee/Artmix **p. 71:**
John Lee/Artmix **p. 75 (top right):** Kathy Klein **p.
79 (top right):** *Mended Spiderweb #8 (Fishpatch),*
1998; courtesy Nina Katchadourian and Catharine
Clark Gallery **p. 86 (top):** Liz Hickok **p. 89 (bottom):**
iStockphoto **p. 90 (clockwise from top to bottom):**
Liza Phillips, Samuel Granados, Kiko Sánchez **p. 91
(clockwise from top right to bottom):** Google Maps;
MAPPING MANHATTAN by Becky Cooper (copyright

© 2013 by Rebecca Cooper, used by permission of
Abrams Image, an imprint of Harry N. Abrams, Inc.,
New York; all rights reserved); Matthew Picton,
2008; **pp. 92–93 (main):** Andy Brandl/Getty Images
p. 93 (top right): NASA **pp. 94–95 (bottom):** Doug
Perrine/SeaPics.com **p. 96 (sand at far left, from
third image down):** John Krzesinski, Jef Poskanzer,
Maria Schoiswohl **p. 97 (bottom):** courtesy Jim
Denevan and Aaron Fee **p. 99 (right):** Amy Snyder
p. 100 (bottom): Edgar Müller **p. 101 (illusions
at far right):** Sumit Mehndiratta **p. 107 (bottom):**
John Lee/Artmix **p. 114 (bottom left):** Georgios
Georgiadis **p. 114 (bottom right):** Jason Edwards/
National Geographic Creative **p. 115 (top):** Richard
T. Nowitz/National Geographic Creative **p. 115
(bottom right):** Steven Bunton **p. 116 (top):** Nemo
Gould **p. 120 (top, clockwise from top to bottom):**
Larry Lynch, Matthew Buckley, Jane Burton/Nature
Picture Library, Mark Britain **p. 121 (bottom):** David
Thoreson **p. 124 (top):** Blend Images/Pete Saloutos/
Getty Images **p. 125 (center right and far right):**
Wikicommons **p. 126 (top):** Christophe Lehenaf/
Getty Images **p. 126 (bottom):** Don Pettit/NASA